C0-AWU-688

The Arnold and Caroline Rose Monograph Series
of the American Sociological Association

Situations and strategies in American land-use planning

Since the 1960s large numbers of American communities have become embroiled in controversies over local land use. The heated nature of the debates suggests the importance of the issues. At the same time a casual reading of rural and suburban newspapers indicates that communities often deal with similar land-use problems in very different ways. *Situations and strategies in American land-use planning* explores these variations in the ways communities resolve land-use problems.

Numerous analyses have identified local land-use controls as the source of our continuing problems with residential segregation and environmental deterioration. Although recent efforts to resolve these problems have focussed on policymaking in local government, the existing literature on land-use control provides little guidance for these efforts. In this context *Situations and strategies in American land-use planning* meets a need. From case studies of regulatory processes in rural, rural–urban fringe, suburban, and urban communities in Connecticut it develops an empirically grounded theory of land-use planning which has clear implications for reforming the local planning process. Thomas Rudel's book will be invaluable to all those involved in planning as well as being of interest to environmental and rural sociologists, geographers, and political scientists concerned with local government.

The Rose Monograph Series was established in 1968 in honor of the distinguished sociologists Arnold and Caroline Rose whose bequest makes the Series possible. The sole criterion for publication in the Series is that a manuscript contribute to knowledge in the discipline of sociology in a systematic and substantial manner. All areas of the discipline and all established and promising modes of inquiry are equally eligible for consideration. The Rose Monograph Series is an official publication of the American Sociological Association.

Editor: Ernest Q. Campbell

Editorial Board:

Andrew Cherlin	Glenn Firebaugh
Daniel Chirot	Virginia Hiday
Phillips Cutright	Teresa Sullivan
Kai Erikson	Jonathan Turner

The Editor and Board of Editors gratefully acknowledge the contributions of Harvey Molotch of the University of California, Santa Barbara, John Logan of the State University of New York, Albany, and John R. Feagin of the University of Texas, Austin, as expert reviewers of this book in manuscript.

For other titles in the series see p. 165.

Situations and strategies in American land-use planning

Thomas K. Rudel

Departments of Human Ecology and Sociology
Rutgers University

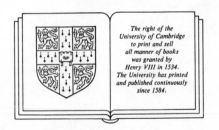

The right of the
University of Cambridge
to print and sell
all manner of books
was granted by
Henry VIII in 1534.
The University has printed
and published continuously
since 1584.

Cambridge University Press

Cambridge

New York   New Rochelle

Melbourne   Sydney

Published by the Press Syndicate of the University of Cambridge
The Pitt Building, Trumpington Street, Cambridge CB2 1RP
32 East 57th Street, New York, NY 10022, USA
10 Stamford Road, Oakleigh, Melbourne 3166, Australia

© Cambridge University Press 1989

First published 1989

Printed in Great Britain at the University Press, Cambridge

British Library cataloguing in publication data
Rudel, Thomas K.
Situations and strategies in American
land-use planning. – (The Arnold and
Caroline Rose monograph series of the
American Sociological Association)
1. United States. Land use. Planning
I. Title II. Series
333.73'0973

Library of Congress cataloguing in publication data
Rudel, Thomas K.
Situations and strategies in American land-use planning/Thomas K. Rudel.
p. cm. – (The Arnold and Caroline Rose monograph series of
the American Sociological Association)
Bibliography.
Includes index.
ISBN 0 521 36186 9
1. Land use – United States – Planning. I. Title II. Series.
HD205.R83 1989
333.73'17'0973–dc19   88-18936

ISBN 0 521 36186 9

UP

333.73170973
R915s

To Susan

Contents

Figures

Tables

Acknowledgements

Funds for the initial period of field research came from a Natural Resources Dissertation Fellowship awarded by Resources for the Future. The New Jersey Agricultural Experiment Station provided funds for a subsequent period of field research. Rutgers University's Faculty Academic Study Program provided financial support, which facilitated the writing up of the results.

Bill Burch provided intellectual stimulus and advice that proved vital to the conduct of this inquiry in its early stages, while Carol McGowan contributed valuable research assistance. I owe a large debt of gratitude to the hundreds of residents and public officials in western Connecticut who took the time to answer my questions about real estate development in their communities. Four people in particular – Louis Goodman of Danbury, Violet Vaill of Goshen, and John and Susan Crockett of Brookfield – provided help during the field research which proved invaluable. In the later stages of this research Peter Pizor and Frank Popper read the entire manuscript and made valuable comments. Harvey Molotch read the manuscript twice and made a series of valuable observations and suggestions. At a critical point in the process of revision Harry Bredemeier made copious comments on the manuscript and pointed out several articles which helped me reformulate my ideas. The editor of the Rose series, Ernest Campbell, and the three reviewers, through a mixture of criticism and encouragement, made me address several issues which measurably improved the manuscript. My warmest appreciation goes to Susan Golbeck, whose support and sensible advice made the writing and rewriting of this manuscript easier in incalculable ways.

1 Introduction: local governments and land-use planning

The purpose of the study

Between 1950 and 1980 the United States experienced a boom in the construction of residential and commercial buildings. Aggregate statistics tell the story. In 30 years developers constructed more than 33 million single-family homes and built more than $561 billion worth of factories, malls, offices, and other non-residential buildings.[1] This boom in building coincided with changes in the geographical distribution of the American population. In massive numbers between 1950 and 1980 Americans moved from cities to suburbs and, more recently, to rural areas (Long, 1981). Under these circumstances developers raised millions of new buildings on tracts of farmland and forest in suburban and rural communities.

This wave of land-use conversion created opportunities and caused problems for a large number of Americans. The opportunities came in the form of increased land values for landowners, improved locations for businesses, and new, well-built, affordable homes for homeowners. The problems involved inadvertent or ill-considered land-use conversions which made it impossible to devote land or buildings to their best use. In Alabama, for example, miners dug coal on lands designated for residential use and reduced the value of nearby homes.[2] In Connecticut a developer built homes in a wetlands which caused the homes to sink and made them uninhabitable.[3] In Florida indiscriminate dredging and filling of wetlands around subdivisions of recreational homes did extensive damage to estuarine life (Allen et al., 1977). In Arizona the construction of subdivision roads on sharply sloped land caused extensive wind erosion (Allen et al., 1976). In each of these instances, officials and residents of the affected communities met to see if they could manage the change from rural to urban land uses more effectively.

The meetings varied widely in tone. At public hearings in Connecticut town halls, local residents gathered to talk about suburbanization. In jam-packed rooms people stood up, one by one, and voiced apprehension about

1

the conversion of their sparsely populated, small town into a densely populated suburb of New York City. The speakers complained about the loss of "peace and quiet" which accompanied suburban development and called upon local officials to reject plans to build more shopping centers, apartment complexes, and residential subdivisions in their towns. In other places the residents stayed home. Lawyers, developers, and zoning commissioners grouped around a set of blueprints in an empty meeting hall and made decisions about land use. The differences in meetings produced differences in policy. In some communities local governments launched time-consuming land-use planning programs which prohibited all intense land uses, including multi-family, low-income housing.[4] In other communities efforts to control land use were ineffectual, especially in cases involving influential local developers.

The contrasts between these communities raise disturbing questions. They convey an impression of regulatory extremism in which communities either permit or prohibit most proposals for development within their jurisdictions. Case studies of land-use planning have contributed to this impression. A series of studies in different settings have documented the absence of effective controls over real estate development (Bernard and Rice, 1983; Feagin, 1983; Molotch, 1976). Other studies, drawing their examples from different places, have outlined a pattern of extensive restriction (Frieden, 1979; Dowall, 1984; Davidoff and Brooks, 1976; Schlay and Rossi, 1981; Williams and Norman, 1974). In the latter communities the regulations, as much as the environmental abuses which they were designed to correct, became the problem. This uneven pattern of regulation prompted numerous reform efforts by higher levels of government during the 1960s and 1970s. Between 1965 and 1976 state legislatures adopted 94 statutes which established minimum standards for local land-use planning in environmentally sensitive areas (Rosenbaum, 1976:31–51). In three northeastern states the courts or the legislatures placed legal limits on the use of local land-use laws for exclusionary purposes (Austin, 1975; Danielson, 1976).

In the 1980s the efforts to circumscribe local control have subsided. Under these circumstances locally initiated reforms offer the only hope for curbing land-use abuses. These reforms will prove workable only if they are founded on an understanding of how communities exercise social control over land use. More precisely, it becomes important to understand the social and ecological conditions which make it possible for communities to establish and enforce norms governing the use of land within their borders. This study uses microsociological approaches to answer this question. It explores the social conditions which give rise to different patterns of land-use planning through an ethnographic study of real estate development and its regulation in a set of western Connecticut communities.

The social control of land use

"Social control refers to all conscious and deliberate attempts to promote conformity to norms" (Gibbs, 1972:2). Efforts to establish social controls over land use usually result in an agreement, with contractual overtones, between a developer and other interested parties which outlines a mutually acceptable change in land use. The interested parties, usually neighboring landowners and commissioners representing the community, exert control over the developer during the process of drawing up the agreements. The type and degree of control exercised by the interested parties varies considerably between communities, but in most places legally enforceable land-use plans are an important instrument of control.

When a community creates a land-use plan, it expresses a vision of how it wants to look in the future, after the conversion of varying amounts of land to urban uses (Garkovich, 1981:51). In effect the plan proposes a set of norms for new land uses in the community. A zoning law enforces these norms by assigning land uses to undeveloped tracts of land. Because the assignment of a land use to a tract of land can have a dramatic impact on the land's value, the drawing of a zoning map involves distributive politics, "the determination of who gets what, where, and how" (Lasswell, 1936, cited in Garkovich, 1981:60). The map determines "where, how much, and what type of growth will occur in the community" (Garkovich, 1981:51). Because land-use planning addresses these distributional questions, it "is more than just another kind of environmental protection. Its goals are too diffuse for that and the social and economic interests it affects are too important" (Healy and Rosenberg, 1979:273).

The impetus to plan almost always comes from developers. They propose to build, and the community reacts to their proposals. The process is not orderly. Land-use authorities, like most other public actors, make decisions in response to pressing problems, and they do so "with haste, poor information, and no theory" (Lynch, 1981:41). If, in a series of deliberations surrounding proposed developments, one group of landowners pushes through provisions favorable to its interests, they establish a set of norms over land use in the community. In other words they establish a system of social control over land use.

Descriptions of local land-use controls

While the literature on land-use planning is voluminous, it sheds little light on differences in controls from community to community. The absence of descriptive accounts reflects the practical orientations of most of the writers. Most students of land-use planning have been either reformers interested in state land-use planning or practitioners (lawyers or planners) interested in the latest trends in land-use law.

While the reformers have identified local land-use controls as a major source of our continuing problems with residential segregation and environmental degradation, they have paid little attention to the social organization of the offending institution. Typically they present the failures in list-like fashion and devote the bulk of their essay to analyses of innovations in state land-use planning. The lack of empirical work on the institution which the reformers hope to change may stem from the frequently held assumption that the impetus for reform in local government must come from the state or federal government. If reform comes from above, with higher levels of government passing laws which prohibit particular provisions in local laws, then analyses of local control need not do more than identify the objectionable provisions.

Descriptions of land-use planning by practitioners usually focus on new planning tools or the latest twist in judicial interpretations. Richard Babcock (1966:xv–xvi) describes the difficulties which this literature poses for anyone interested in patterns of local land-use planning.

In no other field of law is it so difficult to grub out what is taking place from the court decisions, professional journals, and model statutes. A vast amount of decision making is not on record. When it is available, it is often devoted in such detail to the minute facts of individual cases that it is almost impossible to marshal, much less analyze, the bases for decisions.

This emphasis on prescription rather than description serves the purposes of lawyers who want information on new policies or recent court cases, but it causes problems for planners. Citizens frequently complain about "fresh-faced" planners who have a keen understanding of the new state land-use law and little understanding of the locales in which the law must be applied (Berger and Sinton, 1985:152; Eagle, 1976:38; DeGrove, 1979:130; Lassey, 1977:220; Salter, 1981). Having read the literature, the young planners know the content of the new law but not the conditions in which it must be applied.

When observers do make descriptive statements, they are often oversimplified. Economists have been especially diligent in this regard. They have written extensively on the origins and effects of planning and zoning in an attempt to render them intelligible in conventional economic terms. With this reductionist agenda, economists tend toward summary characterizations of local land-use management. They describe zoning as the exercise of monopoly power or the assertion of collective property rights by homeowners (Hamilton, 1978). These characterizations then become the basis for sweeping proposals for reforming zoning law through, for example, the sale of zoning rights (Nelson, 1978). While these general characterizations of land-use control may be more accurate then the summary descriptions produced by other observers, their high level of abstraction reduces their usefulness for explaining intercommunity variations in land-use planning.

The summary descriptions of local land-use planning have another drawback: they frequently contradict one another. For example, the Ralph Nader-sponsored Study Group on Land Use in California refers to local land-use regulators as "the developer's best friend," while Bernard Frieden in a study of northern California suburbs characterizes the same people as uncompromising defenders of pristine suburban environments (Nader, 1973, cited in Popper, 1981:25; Frieden, 1979). In another instance William Fischel writes that "the empirical consensus (among economists) is that zoning allows too little development" (Fischel, 1978:65). The empirical consensus among planners is somewhat different (Conner, 1981:7).

There is little disagreement among planners that traditional zoning has failed to serve the purposes for which it was intended. It consistently fails to protect property values and the environment. It has not even been successful in insulating the hallowed single family home from intrusions by other uses or densities that are too high.

In other words, zoning allows too much development.

Other characterizations of local land-use planning convey an impression of almost random variation. As Richard Babcock (1966:66) writes,

The chaos in land use planning is not the result of uncontrolled individual enterprise. It is a result of a combination of controls and lack of controls, of over-planning and anti-planning, enterprise and anti-enterprise, all in absolute disarray. I doubt that even the most intransigent disciple of anarchy ever wished for or intended the litter that prevails in the area of local land use regulation.

The reluctance of local land-use authorities to base their zoning decisions on a master plan underlines the accuracy of Babcock's observations. As Marion Clawson has noted, about two-thirds of all zoning actions are taken without the guidance provided by a master plan (Clawson, 1975:26). A wide variety of other planners have noted the *ad hoc*, particularistic character of local land-use policy (Hawkins, 1975; Reilly, 1973; Carter *et al.*, 1974). For example, in a widely read essay on local land-use planning, John Reps (1972:12) writes,

Zoning regulations are intensely parochial. Standards required in any single metropolitan area may vary enormously depending on the whims of local legislators...Standards of enforcement vary equally widely. The possibility of achieving coordinated and balanced metropolitan development under such a situation...can be written off as a mere fiction.

The statements about bewildering variations in the law and parochial bases for decision making convey, along with the contradictory characterizations of land-use planning, an impression of tremendous heterogeneity in the social control of land use. Case studies of land-use control reinforce this impression.[5] This book outlines a pattern in the heterogeneity of American land-use planning, presents a theory to explain the pattern, and illustrates the theory with case studies of land-use planning in four disparate types of community. They include a satellite city, a suburb, a rural–urban fringe community, and a rural community. Only large center cities, with their complex redevelopment schemes, lie beyond the purview of this analysis.

Chapter 2 discusses the theory. Chapter 3 describes the setting for the study, with particular attention to the structural shifts in land use and land-use control which occurred when western Connecticut underwent suburban development. This chapter also provides a brief description of the field methods used in the study. Chapters 4, 5, and 6 provide detailed descriptions of how social relations in rural, rural–urban fringe, and urban communities affect processes of land-use control. Chapter 7 assesses the theory and discusses its policy implications.

2 Situations and strategies in local land-use control

Institutions and actors in land-use control

Brief descriptions of the chief institutions and actors involved in land-use planning should provide a convenient point of departure for the more abstract theoretical discussions which follow.

Markets

The theory outlined below begins with the assumption that land-use controls develop in the context of a market for land. As Babcock has observed (1976:39),

Zoning policy and practice are essentially a contest between competing private interests in real estate – the developer or the landowner versus the protesting neighbors and neighboring property owners.

If this portrayal of the interests in land-use control is accurate, then "the image of a free and unorganized market in which individuals compete impersonally for land must be abandoned. This kind of market is highly organized and dominated by a number of interacting organizations" (Form, 1954:33). The social structure of these markets varies in important ways from rural to urban locales. The numbers of buyers and sellers, their financial status, and their knowledge of one another all vary along this dimension. Real estate markets also vary in size. In rural–urban fringe areas a market may extend across six or seven adjacent communities; in more differentiated and densely populated areas they extend over smaller areas.

Developers

A population of developers serves each market. The number and identity of the developers in a market change in predictable ways as places undergo suburban development. In rural communities most developers are locally

7

based; oftentimes they are relatives of the farmers on whose lands they build. Many rural developers build on a part-time basis in a community in which they have resided for many years.

When communities begin to feel the effects of an expanding metropolitan area, land begins to turn over more rapidly; out-of-town landowners increase, and out-of-town developers begin to build in the community (Coughlin, Klein, and Murphy, 1983). With these changes the diversity of developers in a community increases. Out-of-town developers who undertake large projects begin to build alongside local developers who construct two- and three-house subdivisions.

As rural–urban fringe areas become built-up urban places, the developers change again in composition. Large-scale home builders leave the area because they can no longer find the large tracts of land necessary for their projects. The remaining builders specialize in the construction of commercial buildings or small residential subdivisions. They continue to build in the area for long periods of time.

Land users

The predominant type of land user varies dramatically from rural to urban locales. In rural areas economic opportunities usually dictate the land use, and mixed uses are common. A landowner may mine gravel in one corner of his property and pasture cattle on the rest of his land. A resident of the town center may run a store out of the ground floor of his house and live with his family on the second floor. With this pattern of land use, rural landowners often find that they have diffuse or variable interests in land. The storeowner, for example, applauds nearby commercial growth, but he may have second thoughts about growth if the increase in commercial activity impairs the residential ambience of his living quarters. Personal considerations often affect a landowner's reaction to nearby development. Because rural populations are relatively immobile, neighboring landowners have often known one another for long periods of time, and the nature of this relationship can affect the way a neighbor reacts to a proposal to develop land.

As small towns undergo suburban development, individual interests in land change. Builders develop properties for specific commercial, industrial, or residential uses. Given the high cost of developing land for an urban use and the difficulty of converting to another use, property owners usually want to maintain the original use. Under these circumstances owners react to a nearby change in land use solely in terms of its effect on their own specific use. With this agenda suburban property owners tend to view nearby developments with a more critical eye than their rural counterparts do. This change in interests contributes to the creation of sharply defined homeowner and developer interest groups that participate actively in the land-use politics of the more urbanized communities.

Land-use authorities

Communities with land-use laws have elected or appointed officials who administer the laws. These officials sit on commissions which review proposed changes in land use; in the larger communities professional planners assist the commissioners in reviewing proposals. The commissions change in composition as communities undergo suburban development, and these changes affect the policies which the commissioners pursue. In rural and rural–urban fringe places many commissioners are builders, realtors, or farmers; one also finds the occasional commissioner who represents homeowners who commute to work outside the community. Whatever the early commissioners' ideological predispositions, they exercise considerable influence in local land-use politics because they play an important role in drawing up the first land-use law (Rudel, 1980:36). With continued suburban development commissioners who work outside the community and advocate restrictive land-use policies begin to predominate on commissions. This change in the characteristics of the commissioners occurs unevenly across communities. In suburbs almost all the commissioners earn their incomes outside the community and advocate restrictive land-use policies; in satellite cities local realtors and builders retain a presence on commissions. The guidelines of a community's land-use laws limit the range of choices open to the later commissioners, but they can still obstruct or expedite development projects through their control over project reviews. When a developer or his adversaries disagree with a commission's decision, they appeal the decision in the state courts. In these instances a judge becomes the land-use authority.

Land-use controls emerge out of interactions between developers, nearby land users, and land-use authorities. The interested parties contract with one another, sometimes directly, sometimes through the good offices of their local government, on issues of land use. The outcomes vary widely. In some communities there is no land-use policy; aggregations of individuals express their interests informally to one another, and these interactions sometimes lead to modifications in land use. In other communities likeminded landowners with specific norms about land use enact and enforce restrictive land-use laws. In still other communities the laws express norms about land use, but local officials are reluctant to enforce them. These differences in policy follow geographic and socio-economic lines. Most rural communities do not have zoning laws, the most rudimentary of planning tools (Rudel, 1984a). Enacted, but loosely enforced laws are found most frequently in cities and rural–urban fringe communities (Lorimer, 1972; Socolow, 1968). The most restrictive land-use laws are usually found in suburbs (Frieden, 1979; Dowall, 1984). These patterns invite us to develop a "comparative political economy of place" (Logan, 1976b) which relates variations in the configuration of local interests to variations in land-use controls.

Theoretical approaches

Most social scientific work on land-use planning has been devoted to establishing the explanatory primacy of a particular set of variables. One approach argues for the importance of ecological and technological variables while a second approach emphasizes political–economic variables. The two approaches and the contributions they make to understanding the social control of land use are outlined below.

Ecological approach

A long-standing school of thought in human ecology argues that political activities do not have appreciable effects on patterns of land-use regulation because politicians follow market trends in making decisions. The market trends usually begin with technological changes such as the construction of new highways (Hawley, 1950:200; Berry and Kasarda, 1977:191, 196–197). The highways initiate major changes in the value of land by reducing the commuting time between an urban center and outlying communities. As commuter traffic on roads in the outlying communities increases, residentially zoned land fronting on the roads becomes more attractive as sites for commercial development. To obtain the higher prices characteristic of commercially zoned land, landowners along the roads apply to have their land rezoned, and, in this rendition of land-use planning, public officials grant the rezoning requests. In other words trends in the market produce, over time, trends in the regulations (Alonzo, 1965; McBride and Clawson, 1970:22–29; Schmid, 1970). Changes in markets also induce changes in policy through changes in interests groups which occur as development takes place (Park, Burgess, and MacKenzie, 1925:90; Birch, 1971). David Harvey (1973:167–168) describes this process.

The urban area is built up sequentially over a long period of time, and activities and people take up positions in the urban system sequentially. Once located, activities and people tend to be particularly difficult to move... Land use theory then appears as a sequential space packing problem (with the possibility of adding space at the periphery).

In this space packing process "local government... speaks for the people who get there first" (Reilly, 1973:225), but late arrivals do obtain changes in policy. The changes do not occur immediately. In most cases a change in land use, repeated dozens of times on different parcels of land, gradually alters the configuration of interests in a community, and this change in interests causes a change in policy. For example, the steady construction of single-family homes gradually populates rural–urban fringe communities with people who lobby for and eventually obtain restrictive land-use controls for residential areas. In exceptional cases a single conversion to a new use causes a change in the land-use plan. In one western Connecticut community the construction of a large retirement community so altered the political composition of the community that, when the retirees began to attend meetings and vote, they were able to push through significant increases in restrictions over land use. Attempted as well as actual changes in land use shape municipal plans. For example, when a company announced plans to build a slaughterhouse in a rural Connecticut community, the zoning commissioners, without a provision concerning slaughterhouses, quickly created one which prohibited the proposed land use.

The argument that changes in land-use conversion precipitate changes in land-use control has received empirical support in a study in northern California which found more restrictive land-use planning in communities which had experienced more rapid population growth in the preceding ten years (Baldassare and Protash, 1982:343). Recast in more general terms, the adoption of restrictive controls over land use signals a population's adaptation to a changing environment (Berry and Kasarda, 1977:12). Elite groups do not play a prominent role in the creation of new norms about land use; instead, an evolving aggregation of individual interests, expressed through the market, determines land-use policy.

Political–economic approach

The ecological approach with its emphasis on the importance of transportation-induced changes in land-use conversion makes an undeniable contribution to our understanding of how communities regulate real estate development, but questions have arisen as to whether ecological and technological variables can provide a complete explanation of the regulatory process. Critics have focused on the absence of political variables in the ecological approach and have argued that this omission produces explanations which are deficient in two respects. First, because the ecological approach ignores power differentials between the parties interested in land-use change, it fails to appreciate the degree to which elite groups have been able to shape land-use patterns to their own ends. Developers, with extensive ties to financial elites, shape land-use patterns by putting together proposals for new land uses and by manipulating governmental reviews of land-use changes. The developers' influence over the review process has several sources. People with financial connections to the property industry sit, in disproportionate numbers, on local land-use commissions and make decisions which bring the industry economic advantages (Lorimer, 1972:95–134). By making generous campaign contributions, the elites oblige local politicians to work for favorable decisions on the industry's development proposals (Lorimer, 1972:65–79). The evidence documenting the elites' influence and the effects of their influence makes a persuasive case for including political variables in explanations of land-use planning.

The first oversight in ecological accounts of development, involving political groups, appears related to a second oversight involving the salience of political conflict. Developers' proposals to convert areas to new uses usually threaten local residents, and in these instances conflict breaks out between the two groups. The events which trigger conflict are quite varied. Road construction projects (Amir, 1972), airport expansions (Nelkin, 1974), gentrification (Holcomb and Beaureguard, 1981), and low-income housing (Davidoff and Brooks, 1976) have all precipitated conflicts over land use. If the outcomes of the conflicts always favored the elites, one might be able to justify overlooking the conflicts on the grounds that they do nothing more than delay land-use changes. While elites win most disputes, they lose others, such as the recent Westway controversy in New York City. Each win or loss has a visible impact on local land use; construction occurs or it does not. In this way differences between places in the incidence and outcomes of conflict contribute to differences in land-use patterns. In this light the neglect of land-use conflicts in ecological explanations of the planning process would appear to be a serious oversight.

Attempts to incorporate political inequalities and conflict into explanations of real estate development have taken two forms. Several theorists, working at a high level of aggregation, have outlined the political economy of urban development under capitalism; other analysts, working at much lower levels of aggregation, have provided detailed case studies of how political-economic processes have shaped real estate development in particular cities or sets of cities. The work of Manuel Castells, David Harvey, and Allen Scott provide prominent examples of the first type of political economic analysis.

Castells' work (1977, 1983) has focused on the large, somewhat amorphous phenomenon of urban social change. He has developed a theory of urban social change which conceives of cities as "arenas for collective consumption" (Gottdeiner, 1985:138) and focuses on inequalities in the provision of collective goods and conflicts between consumption classes. This theoretical framework, while impressive in its logic, works better in some applications than in others. Applied to land-use changes, Castells' framework has particular difficulty with the behavior of developers (Gottdeiner, 1985:140). Homeowners and developers struggle over a consumption good – housing – but developers hardly can be considered a consumption group. Castells' theory of how user groups behave requires a complementary theory of how developers behave before it can claim to be a comprehensive theory of urban land-use change.

Two other theorists, David Harvey (1973, 1981) and Allen Scott (1980), provide political–economic explanations for urban land development. Their works feature skeletal descriptions of processes of urban development followed by complex reconceptualizations of Marxist theory which, in revised form, account for the observed processes. The lengthy theoretical discussions in their work elucidate the connections between urban development and the larger economy, but inadequacies in their descriptions of urban development diminish the value of this work for students of land-use planning. The empirical shortcomings in Harvey's and Scott's work are most evident in their descriptions of interest groups and conflict. Harvey and Scott identify two groups interested in urban development, a capitalist class faction which develops land and an urban proletariat which defends neighborhoods against incursions by developers. Land-use conflicts, which are almost always clashes between these two groups, are therefore instances of class conflict. The conflicts are ubiquitous, an ever-present aspect of urban development.

This characterization of land-use conflicts has not gone unchallenged. A number of observers (Gottdeiner, 1985:165–170) have noted that the developers' adversaries are frequently affluent homeowners who do not fit the description of a proletariat. Questions have arisen about the incidence of land-use conflict and in particular the assertion that it is an ubiquitous phenomenon. As a number of observers have pointed out (Lorimer, 1972:194; Molotch, 1976:311), the interactions between developers and local residents are variable, sometimes involving conflict and sometimes involving cooperation. In sum, this group of theorists places a welcome emphasis on political processes in real estate development, but neither they nor their students have gone on to produce full-bodied accounts of how individuals, interest groups, and governments interact in the conversion of land to new uses.

Working outside the confines of a self-conscious theoretical tradition, a mixed group of planners, journalists, and sociologists has produced a series of detailed, almost ethnographic, accounts of how political–economic processes shape real estate development in metropolitan areas. These studies have varied in focus and locale. Chester Hartman's studies of San Francisco (1974, 1984) and James Lorimer's studies of Canadian cities (1972, 1979) have focused on the development of downtown districts. Robert Caro (1974) looked at public works construction in the New York metropolitan area; Pierre Clavel's (1986) study focused on the development and redevelopment activities of progressive city governments in five small to middle-sized American cities; Joe Feagin's study of Houston (1985) stressed the influence of external factors, such as changes in the world oil economy, on the development of Houston. Mark Gottdeiner (1977) demonstrated how a political economic configuration which included weak political parties, unorganized homeowners, and large-scale developers produced ineffectual planning along Long Island's rural–urban fringe.

Several similarities run through this body of work. First, all the authors take a historical approach to the study of real estate development. This approach acknowledges the unique circumstances which accompany each project. More important, by examining how individual projects evolve through time, these studies underline how each project involves a complicated pulling and hauling between interest groups who pursue strategies which change over time. In so doing, the narrative accounts capture the dynamic aspect of the development process. Secondly, all of the historical studies make clear the importance of political inequalities in explaining outcomes in real estate development. While one might be tempted upon reading these studies to conclude, somewhat mechanistically, that the politically powerful always prevail, the histories are too complex to permit such a simple interpretation. For example, the history of the Yerba Buena redevelopment project in San Francisco becomes comprehensible only when one realizes that the setting for much of the conflict, a federal court, reduced the tremendous disparities in power between the contending parties, influential developers and elderly renters threatened with displacement.

While the emphasis on political–economic dynamics in the narrative accounts of real estate development improves our understanding of urban development, a lack of variation in the communities under study limits this literature's usefulness as a source for an explanation of variations in land-use planning. Perhaps because rapid or large-scale real estate development raises particularly pressing policy questions, the foci for the case studies have been places, usually cities but occasionally rural–urban fringe communities (Gottdeiner, 1977; Feagin, 1983:140–173), characterized by rapid or large-scale development.[1] Inner suburbs and rural communities, places where development occurs at a slow rate or is small in scale, are underrepresented in this literature.

The theories which use the narrative accounts as a basis for generalization have difficulty explaining patterns of development in the underrepresented communities. For example, Feagin (1983) argues that urban real estate development can be likened to the game of Monopoly, a zero-sum game in which the rich win and the poor lose. This analogy makes sense in urban real estate development where new construction almost always involves displacement, with the rich moving in and the poor being pushed out. The analogy seems less useful in rural areas where development usually involves the conversion of agricultural lands to an urban use and rarely involves displacement. A comprehensive theory of land-use planning must be able to explain patterns of land-use planning in the less-studied as well as more-studied places.

Fortunately, Harvey Molotch has elaborated a model of the political economy of urban development which has the specificity lacking in other theories and the potential for application across a wide range of communities. In a 1976 article Molotch described cities as "growth machines" run by land-based elites for their own economic advantage. His model has two somewhat contradictory features. First, he considers cities to be "growth machines." The analogy to a machine seems apt because the elite coalitions which dominate local politics are multipartite political entities which pursue economic growth in an unvarying, indefatigable way. Secondly, while local elites coalesce to attract investors to a community, they also compete over the shape or location of projects within a community. Given these contingencies, Molotch argues that each locality should be regarded "as a mosaic of competing land interests capable of strategic coalition and action" (1976:310).

The growth-machine theory should prove to be useful for understanding land-use planning because it models activities which are an integral part of the land-use planning process. Land-use planning brings developers together with other interested parties, some of whom may oppose a particular project;

under these circumstances the deliberations which surround land-use planning should provide frequent examples of growth coalitions at work.[2] In addition to being pertinent, Molotch's model appears to be applicable across a wide range of American communities. In a study of 25 American cities Lyon and his associates (1981) found, as the growth-machine model would predict, an association between the dominance of pro-business elites and population growth in a place. McGranahan (1984) provided further support for the model in a study of rural communities in Wisconsin. He found that the aggressive pursuit of extralocal influentials by local elites associated positively with population growth in a place. Other studies (Krannich and Humphrey, 1983; Maurer and Christenson, 1982) have specified variations in the way growth machines operate.

The growth-machine model has several applications to land-use planning phenomena. One is simple and straightforward; the other is circuitous. In its simple application, growth-machine theory would predict that, because pro-growth elites dominate local politics everywhere, communities should relinquish control over land use whenever their regulations conflict with elite interests. This understanding of land-use planning shares with the ecological approach the assumption that land-use commissions are permeable institutions, but in this approach political inequalities rather than market forces determine the policies which land-use authorities pursue.

While this application of Molotch's model has the virtues of simplicity, it suffers from a serious defect. It implicitly argues that, because pro-business elites dominate everywhere, land-use planning must be uniformly ineffective. This presumption does not square with the patterns of land-use planning outlined in chapter 1. In many communities pro-business elites dominate land-use planning, but in other places, white-collar suburbs for instance, anti-growth coalitions dominate the land-use planning process (Baldassare and Protash, 1982).

Molotch and Logan (1984) offer an explanation for this anomaly, and in so doing, they suggest a second, more fruitful application of the growth-machine model. Molotch and Logan argue that in the past 20 years local elites have lost their autonomy as large corporations captured a progressively larger share of product markets. The individual who runs a local manufacturing plant is now a branch plant manager rather than an independent proprietor. In addition to a change in the characteristics of the economic elite, the scale of proposed projects and the environmental damage associated with them have increased. The absence of local ties among the new elites and the environmental costs of their projects facilitate the formation of countervailing coalitions among local residents. To defend their community against ambitious development projects, these coalitions push through restrictive land-use planning laws.

While the empirical validity of this explanation for restrictive land-use planning remains open to question, the analytic strategy employed by Molotch and Logan suggests a comprehensive explanation of patterns in American land-use planning. In Molotch's original (1976) discussion he stressed that interactions between local elite groups are fluid, that they change over time and from project to project. This emphasis is evident in Molotch and Logan's (1984) argument. A change in the characteristics of one elite group (elite delocalization) alters the pattern of interaction between interest groups in a way that yields a new set of land-use policies. Extending this analytic strategy to land-use planning, one might argue that changes in the character and composition of local interest groups along with changes in the pattern of interaction between them should explain changes in land-use planning.

With the exception of Molotch's work most political–economic analyses pay only rudimentary attention to the patterns of interaction between interest groups. Interest groups provide the building blocks in the political economic approach, but discussions of interest group interactions are limited to observations that class-based interest groups conflict with one another. Variations in the way interest groups interact receive little attention. This processual variable is important for understanding land-use planning because regulations do not spring fully armed from the collective imaginations of interest groups. Rather the exercise of control over land use involves a process in which the interested parties interact over time. Variations in the composition of the parties and the conditions under which they interact give rise to variations in the terms of agreement, the costs of reaching agreement, and the effectiveness of agreed-upon arrangements about land use. A marriage of these processual considerations with the structural variables identified in the political–economic and ecological approaches should produce a more complete explanation of how land-use planning works in the United States.

Combining structure and process in the study of land-use planning

The incorporation of processual variables into explanations of land-use planning requires that we trace out the effects of structural variables on interactions between the parties interested in land use. James S. Coleman (1966) has suggested one such link. He argues that the likelihood of collective action diminishes when an action is not part of a sequence of collective actions. When collective actions are part of a sequence, actors will agree to actions which interest them little in order to obtain agreement from others on actions which interest them more. This argument has a straightforward application to the interactions between developers and neighboring landowners. In residentially stable rural communities with low rates of land-use conversion adjacent landowners will anticipate longterm relationships with one another. They expect to undertake unspecified but conceivably important joint actions in the future, and this expectation gives them incentives to arrive at informal agreements about current land-use issues. In rural–urban fringe communities with their high rates of land-use conversion and more transient populations, the interested parties anticipate a temporary relationship, so the likelihood of agreements about land use would be lower. In urban communities with their lower rates of land-use conversion and less transient populations of developers the likelihood of agreement should be somewhat higher.

In recent years game theorists have extended Coleman's argument. The usefulness of their work depends in large measure on the accuracy of the claim that land-use conversion resembles a game. The analogy to a game has been made several times. In the best-known book on American land-use planning, Richard Babcock (1966) made the point twice, in the title (*The Zoning Game*) and in the table of contents, which he organized into two sections, part one on players and part two on rules. Despite these signposts, Babcock never explained why land-use planning could be considered a game and did not draw upon game theory in his analyses of land-use planning. Joe Feagin titled his recent book *The Urban Real Estate Game* (1983) and likened urban real estate development to the game of Monopoly, but he did not explain why urban land-use conversion could be considered a game.

Detailed descriptions of land-use politics make the empirical basis for this claim clear. Norton Long (1958) describes the planning process associated with the construction of a highway as "a complicated pulling and hauling" between economically interdependent actors. Molotch describes the basis for interdependence in real estate development:

any given locality is an aggregate of land based interests...each landowner has in mind a certain future for a parcel that is linked somehow with his or her own well being. If there is a simple ownership the relationship is straightforward: to the degree to which the lands' profit potential is enhanced, one's own wealth is increased...More subtle is the emergence of concern for an aggregate of parcels: one sees that one's future is bound to the future of a larger area, that the future enjoyment of financial benefit flowing from a given parcel will derive from the general future of the proximate aggregate of parcels. (Molotch, 1976:310–311)

The interdependence described by Molotch is the defining characteristic of a game. According to Morganstern (1968:62), games take place when

each participant is striving for his greatest advantage in situations where the outcome depends not only on his actions alone, nor solely on those of nature, but also on those of other participants whose interests are sometimes opposed, sometimes parallel to his own.

The interdependence of outcomes makes strategic considerations important in games. The strategies are based on expectations about the actions of other interested parties. Long (1958:253) illustrates this point in his discussion of highway construction:

...the interrelationship of the groups in constructing a highway has been developed over time, and there are general expectations as to the interaction...There are...generalized expectations as to how politicians, contractors, newspapermen, bankers, and the like will utilize the highway situation...In fact the knowledge that a banker will play like a banker and a newspaperman like a newspaperman is an important part of what makes the situation calculable and permits the players to estimate its possibilities for their own action

Because each actor's reward depends on the actions of others, he will maximize his rewards if he can anticipate the actions of other players and devise a plan of action which enables him to benefit from their actions. In Jon Elster's words "the reward of each depends on the choice of all" (1982:464). This situation certainly characterizes adjacent landowners in areas undergoing real estate development. These observations suggest that game theory may help explain interactions between landowners as they struggle in an evolving context to benefit from changes in land use.

There are many varieties of game theory, most of which are not useful for our purposes because the situations they embody do not resemble land-use conversion situations. One class of games, referred to as social dilemmas, embody some of the basic features of land-use conversion situations. Although social dilemma games can be modelled in several different ways, they usually have two players who cannot communicate with one another. Many land-use conversion situations in suburban and rural locales have two principal players, a developer and nearby property owners. Although communication between the developer and adjacent property owners is always possible, it is by no means assured. Most crucially, the configuration of payoffs in social dilemmas and land-use conversion situations is similar. In most instances of land-use conversion, the use which would bring the most money to the developer has more negative spillover effects on adjacent residents than a less lucrative land use would have. In these instances individual and collective interests diverge, creating a social dilemma. Three games (the prisoner's dilemma, chicken, and trust) present participants with this dilemma (Liebrand, 1983; Zagare, 1984:52). The highest collective payoff comes from cooperation, but a strategy of defection from cooperative solutions yields a higher individual payoff except in those instances where both players defect. When the payoffs take this configuration, "uncoordinated decision-making by selfish maximizers will produce a suboptimal outcome" (Orbell and Wilson, 1978:412).

Before we proceed further a cautionary note is in order. The payoffs to participants in land-use conversion are too variable and too difficult to measure to say with certainty that the interested parties face a configuration of payoffs which characterizes one rather than another of the social dilemma games. Fortunately the theory reviewed below, while developed to explain behaviors in a prisoner's dilemma, appears to apply to other social dilemmas as well (Axelrod, 1984:221; Maynard Smith, 1982).

Recent simulation studies of the prisoner's dilemma have focused on the length of the game. If a game is short, consisting of only one round of play, participants usually do not engage in cooperative behavior (Hardin, 1982:16–124; Axelrod, 1984:7–10). If the game is long, consisting of many rounds of play, the players participate in an iterated prisoner's dilemma. Under these circumstances participants will take the future actions of other players into account in deciding what to do. In particular they will choose cooperative behavior in the present round of play in hopes of inducing cooperative behavior in other players in subsequent rounds of play (Axelrod, 1984:3–24, 55–68). These findings confirm Coleman's earlier, more general contentions.

Game theorists pay particular attention to the strategies pursued by individual players. Axelrod demonstrates that players who follow 'tit-for-tat' strategies accumulate more points in a series of games than do players who use other strategies. Players who follow tit-for-tat strategies can be considered nice players because they start with a cooperative move; in subsequent rounds of play they do what the other player did on the previous round of play. These players consistently outscore players who begin by defecting because numerous nice players receive the higher cooperative payoffs (R) in the later rounds while defectors receive the lower punishment payoffs (P). The success of the tit-for-tat strategy underscores the contention that parties who reciprocate cooperative behaviors will work out agreed upon solutions to social dilemmas in the absence of a central authority.

On issues of land use an individual's anticipated as well as actual length of residence may provide the most direct analogue to the length of a game or the length of a sequence of collective actions.[3] Given the logic outlined above, this variable should explain a set of behaviors among participants in land-use conversion. Among immobile residents the shadow of future relations with one another gives them incentives to cooperate on issues of land use. By extension, residents with a long-term commitment to an area should rely more than other residents on informal discussions to resolve problems. Survey research provides some empirical support for this expectation. In a recent study of middle- and lower-class neighborhoods in Seattle, Guest and Lee (1983:228) found that long length of residence associated positively with informal interactions with neighbors.

Other findings from the simulation studies take Coleman's argument further. Axelrod demonstrates that clusters of cooperating players can persist in a population where a majority of the players tend to defect. A similar spatial patterning may characterize the informal controls which adjacent landowners exert over one another. The clusters of cooperating landowners should be distributed nonrandomly, even in a population where everyone is a long-term resident. Where considerable inequalities in power exist between adjacent landowners, tit-for-tat strategies are unlikely to develop, and the threat of retaliatory action will not deter the powerful landowner from going ahead with a change in land use. These considerations suggest that clusters of cooperating players will develop only in places where landowners enjoy relatively equal amounts of power.

These observations about the likelihood of cooperation across types of players and situations can be recast in dynamic terms. If, for example, structural changes increase the mobility of participants in a real estate market, a decline in the prevalence of voluntary solutions to land-use problems should follow. In general this theoretical excursion suggests the empirical outlines of social structures which promote cooperation or conflict between landowners. The incidence of cooperation or conflict among developers and other interested parties should in turn affect the form of land-use control which a community adopts.

Two forms of control stand out in the literature on governance structures (MacNeil, 1974, 1978; Williamson, 1979, 1981). One type we might call relational control because the social pressures exerted in face to face encounters figure centrally in this form of control. Relational control appears in bilateral and trilateral forms. In the bilateral form the interested parties negotiate directly with one another; in the trilateral form the two interested parties meet with a third party who contributes to the resolution of any disagreements, in some cases through mediation, in other cases through the exercise of legal authority. Rules provide the foundation for another type of control. With rule-based controls the parties interested in a change in land use present their case to a commission which measures the proposed change against a standard established by law. Over time the commission applies the law to a succession of proposed changes in land use.

Relational and rule-based controls represent different ways of arriving at agreements. Reflection about the different forms of control suggests that each one will minimize the costs of reaching and enforcing agreements about land use under somewhat different conditions. Bilateral relational control reduces transaction costs to a minimum; the neighboring landowners get together and talk over a proposed change in land use, but no one is legally obliged to carry out an agreement. To be effective, neighboring landowners must feel a sense of obligation to one another. The theory of cooperation suggests that this pattern of control should be especially prevalent in residentially stable rural areas where neighbors have relatively equal amounts of power, are long-time acquaintances, and expect to interact on numerous occasions in the future. Rule-based control where a commission applies a simple law to a series of proposed changes in land use has the advantage of being legally enforceable. It would appear to be useful in circumstances in which landowners have strong incentives to convert to land uses which have damaging spillover effects. This pattern of control should characterize rural–urban fringe areas because, with the rapid turnover of real estate in these areas, relationships between neighboring landowners tend to be transitory, so the incentive to cooperate is weak. This circumstance, coupled with the rising land prices, increases the temptation to convert to intense, profit-making land uses with negative spillover effects. Trilateral relational control features planners who mediate disputes and judges who hand down decisions. It adds a relational dimension to a pre-existing set of rule-based controls. Because trilateral relational control includes third parties who specialize in dispute resolution, it is likely to emerge in urban areas where nearly every proposed change in land use gives rise to a dispute. Because the conflicts are iterative, with the same developers encountering similar groups of hostile homeowners each time they propose to build, the developers learn to expect conflict. Under these circumstances the shadow of the future looms large, and cooperative behavior in the form of negotiations between developers and potentially hostile groups such as homeowner associations or land use commissioners may begin.

These relationships between places and patterns of control are spelled out in more detail below.

Bilateral controls and slow-growing rural areas

Bilateral relational controls over land use involve informal agreements between neighboring landowners. The activities of Laurence Rockefeller in a Catskill valley, approximately 120 miles northwest of New York City, provide one example of this form of control. A neighbor of Mr. Rockefeller's described the system of control.

Larry will go around the valley, and, if he sees something he thinks is unattractive, he'll ask people if they'd change it, and he'll pay to have it fixed up.[4]

Clearly Mr. Rockefeller's practice is exceptional in his willingness to pay for changes in his neighbors' land use, but in its essentials it is like other, less-noted efforts by neighbors to influence each other's use of land. Neighbors arrive at these agreements through face-to-face negotiations. Aside from exceptional cases, these agreements are not legally binding. For their effectiveness they rely on the shadow of the future (Axelrod, 1984: 126–132). Because the parties to agreements have relatively low rates of residential mobility and make some economic use of their land, they assume that they will want to ask for each other's cooperation on both trivial and important matters in the future. With this expectation it becomes important to remain in good standing with one's neighbors; one way to do this is to observe informal agreements about land use.

As noted above, the tit-for-tat strategies which support informal controls are most effective when low rates of residential mobility and land-use conversion prevail in a place. Under these circumstances, the ownership of most tracts of land will not change in the near future. The accompanying view of stability in rural land markets works against efforts to establish alternative systems of control. Ann Strong (1975:167) outlines this connection in her analysis of an effort to reform land-use laws in rural Pennsylvania.

Most [residents] did not feel any pressures from urbanization and did not believe anything would happen for another twenty years...To people who had barely accepted zoning, we were proposing a major invasion of their right to control the use of their land. Most simply were not persuaded that the circumstances required such drastic action...we could produce no crises to which our planning would be one response...None of us knew how we could have stimulated widespread local interest in planning for the Upper East Branch in the absence of a real or artificially generated crisis.

In this setting informal agreements between landowners seem sufficient to control the occasional small changes in land use which occur. Because the agreements are informal, evidence for their existence is hard to find. Farmers in southern New Jersey arrive at agreements within their families which limit the construction of homes for the younger generation to agriculturally unproductive lands (Berger and Sinton, 1985:97). A study of the administration of land-use laws in Iowa alludes to the informal controls over land use which operate in communities without zoning (Iowa, 1977). Other reports from places as diverse as Arizona, Wyoming, and Minnesota note how the presence of a pre-existing system of informal controls complicates the enforcement of recently enacted zoning laws (Eagle, 1976; Minnesota, 1981; Nellis, 1980).

Rules and rapidly growing rural–urban places

The incorporation of a rural community into an expanding metropolitan area increases the rate of land-use conversion and alters landowners' interests (Parker *et al.*, 1984, Schmid, 1970). These changes increase the attractiveness of short-term, profit-seeking behavior and, in so doing, reduce the effectiveness of informal controls over land use. Accelerating rates of real estate development raise the price of land which increases the attractiveness of selling out to the highest bidder, no matter what the proposed land use (Coughlin, Klein, and Murphy, 1983). Changes in market conditions induce opportunistic behaviors; landowners renege on promises to maintain a particular land use, and realtors exaggerate the stability of local land-use patterns in conversations with prospective homeowners.[5] The rapid growth rates attract builders who are both new to the profession (Kenney, 1972) and new to the community. With little attachment to the place or the profession, these builders feel little obligation to maintain a particular standard of work in their projects. In other words rapid growth introduces incentives which, by raising the mobility of land users, destroys the recurrent relationships which make bilateral relational controls effective.

By giving legal force to prohibitions on locally unwanted land uses, rule-based controls prevent certain types of land-use conversions. Some landowners, who might have made a particularly noxious use of their land in the absence of a law, decide to use their land differently. Other landowners avoid objectionable uses only if they see the law being enforced. Because most communities allocate only small sums of money for enforcement, only large changes in land use, with corresponding potentials for abuse, receive any oversight. Minor changes, such as the creation of a small dump on a farm, usually get no attention from the regulators. Other factors limit the scope of the laws. Because the politics of communities experiencing rapid development are usually dominated by "growth coalitions" of local businessmen who oppose restrictions which might limit development, the laws are incomplete. Developers exploit these omissions by proposing land uses for which the laws have no regulatory guidelines. Under these circumstances planners scramble to update the laws while developers hurry to file under the old, more permissive laws. Despite the laws' limited scope some developers seek exemption from them through illegal means. Although the nature of this activity makes it impossible to determine its frequency, several studies have argued that attempts to corrupt land-use authorities are particularly frequent in rapidly growing communities (Clawson, 1971; Law Enforcement Assistance Administration, 1979:29–37).

By attracting outside developers to fringe areas, the rapid rates of land-use conversion indirectly facilitate rule by law. Because a growing proportion of developers come from outside the community, a growing proportion of the interactions in the regulatory arena involve developers and land-use commissioners who are relative strangers to one another. 'Special' circumstances founded on a long history of relations between a developer and a commissioner are less likely to arise in these relationships which makes proposals easier to evaluate in the universalistic terms required by law. The ample supply of buildable land eliminates another source of problems in the administration of a law. With extensive tracts of farmland available for development, developers rarely propose to build on lands with extraordinary ecological characteristics, such as wetlands, which would require extensive planning. Similarly the absence of residential subdivisions near most tracts of land slated for development reduces the probability of development induced spillover effects which would require special attention from the authorities.[6] In this context rules expedite the process of control. Laws provide simple standards which make it possible for commissioners meeting on a voluntary basis to evaluate large numbers of proposals in a limited period of time.

Conflict and trilateral controls in slow-growing urban places

Over time the accumulation of buildings in an area creates a situation which is conducive to conflict over land uses. The rising price of land changes the developers' interests. The increased size of investments in land makes it necessary to plan developments which make intense use of land. Invariably these projects involve large sums of money, and developers spend liberally to see their projects approved. If a commission turns down a developer's proposal, he will persist in his attempts to build, either by returning to the commission with a revised proposal or by appealing the commission's decision in the courts. At the same time a change in the land-use pattern facilitates the expression of opposition to the developers' plans. Commercial spots grow into commercial strips, and the enterprises which do business in these places grow larger. Each enterprise occupies more space, serves more customers, and, in so doing, creates spillover effects which discourage the construction of single-family homes nearby. Under these circumstances developers build residential and commercial properties in separate places, and distinct zones of residential and commercial land use emerge. The emergence of zones makes it easier to organize opposition to a development among nearby land users. The similarity in land uses among homeowners gives them a common interest, and, with the impetus provided by proposals to develop nearby tracts of land, homeowners create residential associations to express their interests. The creation of neighborhood organizations becomes easier as neighborhoods grow older. In a new subdivision neighbors have difficulty undertaking collective action because they do not know one another. In time neighbors become acquainted, and these informal ties facilitate the formation of an association. Controversies end, but the residential associations remain in existence, ready to represent homeowners when another proposed development threatens their interests. As neighborhood organizations accumulate over time, local populations become easier to mobilize (Olson, 1982:38–41).

These changes in interest groups alter the political context in which local land-use authorities work. Rather than facing small scale developers and an occasional *ad hoc* group of homeowners as do land-use authorities in more rural areas, authorities in urban communities usually contend with well-financed developers on one side and well-organized homeowners on the other side. Under these circumstances the process of regulation becomes dialectical in form (Schnaiberg, 1984). One party takes action, submits a proposal for a development or a new set of regulations, and the other party responds to their opponent's action.

The probability that a development will have conflict inducing spillover effects increases as communities become more built-up. A growing proportion of the lands to be developed border on built-up tracts of land, usually single-family homes. Because homeowners, like other highly specialized land users, are quick to imagine negative spillover effects from changes in nearby land uses, the increase in the proportion of proposed developments with residential neighbors increases the likelihood that a project will arouse apprehension. Because homeowners have an organizational vehicle for voicing their complaints and developers have a large investment to protect, the two sides do not hesitate to defend their interests.

The decline in the number of real estate developments as communities become more built up reduces the number of occasions for conflict, but the probability of conflict on each occasion rises.

At the same time that landowners show a growing inclination to disagree publically about proposed land uses, changes in the physical setting of development reduce the value of rule-based controls as a means of discriminating between acceptable and unacceptable projects. With increasing proportions of the adjacent tracts of land in an intense use and increasing proportions of the undeveloped land in environmentally sensitive locales, the number of potential land-use abuses is large, and rules cannot anticipate all of them (Bardach and Kagan, 1983:123). To discriminate between developments which do or do not generate damaging spillover effects, land-use authorities add new provisions to their laws, making them more fine grained in their application. Despite these changes the rules frequently fail to provide guidance. In these instances a commission's decisions may depend on the commissioners' estimates about the magnitude of well-known or heretofore unimagined spillover effects. The difficulty of projecting these impacts make it easy, after a decision is handed down, for the losing side to interpret a decision as arbitrary and appeal it in the courts.

As the probability grows that each land-use change will provoke a dispute, a system of trilateral relational controls emerges to decide on land-use changes. In this system developers, homeowners, and other interested parties exchange views about a project in front of authorities who either mediate or pass judgment on the dispute. Because the contending organizations have the resources to challenge adverse decisions, the courts resolve an increasing proportion of all disputes. The arena for decision making shifts from the legislative setting of elected commissions, where interest groups wield considerable power and conflict between them may be inconclusive, to the judicial setting of the state courts where interest groups have less power and decisions about developments are final (DiMento, 1982).

Over time the expense of legal conflict encourages attempts at other forms of trilateral control. As communities become more built-up, the number of authorities who pass judgment on a proposal grows (Bosselman, Feurer, and Sieman, 1976), and the number of interested parties increases. These changes increase the probability of time-consuming and expensive disputes (Frieden, 1979). To minimize the costs of conflict, elected officials encourage their planners to play a mediating role between homeowners and developers. Because developers also want to avoid the expense of court challenges, they may cooperate with local planners in trying to negotiate an acceptable plan of development with the homeowners. In this enterprise the "shadow of the future" in the form of expensive legal proceedings provides the primary impetus behind cooperative efforts.

Trilateral controls characterize land-use changes in both cities and suburbs, but, because the balance of power between interested parties varies from cities to suburbs, land-use conflicts concern different issues and cooperation occurs in different places in the two types of community. In homeowner dominated suburbs the disputes concern threats to homeowners from proposed changes in land use; in developer-dominated cities disputes frequently concern the costs to homeowners of defects in recently constructed homes. In suburbs developers make cooperative gestures toward interested homeowner associations; in cities developers occasionally make similar gestures; more frequently cooperation takes the form of collusion between developers and land-use commissioners with new homeowners bearing the costs of these arrangements. As suburbs and satellite cities diverge in their socio-economic composition during the course of suburban development, these differences in policymaking should grow more extreme.

Summary

The difficulties of reaching agreement about the acceptability of land-uses changes during suburban development, and these changes explain why communities in rural, rural–urban fringe, and urban areas rely on different institutions for controlling the use of land. A series of structural changes, outlined in figure 1, begin to explain why problems of cooperation in land-use conversion change during the course of suburban development. Individuals with a mixture of interests in land and personal interests in each other evolve into landowners with more specialized 'homeowner' or 'developer' interests. The declining distance between land users and the growing intensity with which they use land increases their sensitivity to each other and encourages the creation of zones of land use. The landscape takes on a 'patchy' appearance, and over time these patches generate politically mobilized user groups which contend with developers in the political arena. Developers also change. As a wave of land-use conversion begins in an area, developers become more numerous, more varied in their backgrounds, and more opportunistic in their building practices. As the wave of conversions subsides, the number of developers declines, and those who continue to build become more willing, albeit to a greater extent in suburbs than in cities, to negotiate with nearby homeowners about the substance of their projects. Theories of how interested parties interact suggest that these changes should

	Slow-growing rural areas	Fast-growing rural–urban fringe areas	Slow-growing or declining areas in the metro core
Location, land market			
Communities richer	Exurban communities	Exurbs	Suburbs
Communities poorer	Farming communities	Residential, commercial centers	Satellite cities
Extent of developed land	Low .... High		
Land users	Less specialized, less intense		More specialized, more intense
Developers	Small, locally based developers	Out-of-town developers enter market	Local developers, large and small, predominate
Landscape	Spots of urban land uses mixed among rural uses		Zones emerge: areas of urban land use take on patchy appearance
Conflict	Low incidence of conflict over land-use change		High incidence of conflict over land-use change
Land-use control	Bilateral relational controls	Rule-based controls	Trilateral relational controls

Figure 1 *Structural shifts associated with changes in land-use planning during suburban development The dotted lines indicate a continuum along a dimension. The increasing density of the line dividing the two types of communities as it moves from left to right denotes increasing differences in land-use planning policies between communities at the same stage of development.*

produce in succession three situationally appropriate patterns of land-use control, bilateral relational control for rural areas, rule-based control for rural–urban fringe areas, and trilateral relational control for urban areas. The following chapters explore the empirical bases for these hypotheses through a field study of processes of land-use control in western Connecticut communities.

3 Suburban development and land-use planning in western Connecticut

The sample of communities

Any claim to comprehensiveness in a study of local land-use control rests on the adequacy of the sample of communities selected for study. The typology outlined in figure 1 guided the selection of communities for study. To explore the cumulative effects of development, I needed communities at the three major stages of development, so the study included rural as well as rural–urban fringe and urban communities. Because socio-economic differentiation between communities becomes most apparent in the built-up areas of a metropolitan region, it seemed possible to ignore socio-economic differences between communities at earlier but not later stages of real estate development. These considerations argued for case studies in four communities. Of the four communities two would be peripheral communities at different stages of development, a rural community and a rural–urban fringe community, and two would be highly differentiated core communities, an established suburb and an adjoining satellite city.[1]

The region selected for study had to contain a wide range of variation in real estate development. This criterion ruled out southern and western regions where the metropolitan areas frequently do not contain slow-growing communities in the urban core. Northeastern and North Central regions looked better on this criterion. In addition to slow-growing rural communities beyond the fringes of metropolitan areas, the older regions had rapidly growing fringe areas as well as slow-growing or declining areas in urban centers. On this basis a sample of communities in the northeastern or north central United States seemed most appropriate.[2]

State land-use policies also influenced the selection of a region for study. These policies vary considerably from state to state, and their impact on local land-use policies varies accordingly. In order to prevent differences in state policies from introducing additional variation into local land-use policies, the region selected for study could not extend across state boundaries. It also seemed advisable to choose a region within a state which did not have

31

restrictive enabling legislation. For example, by requiring that all communities adopt land-use laws which conform to state approved master plans, New Jersey eliminates much of the variation in land-use policy which I wanted to examine. A suitable region for study had to be part of an older metropolitan area in a state which grants most of its regulatory powers over land use to local governments. A number of areas outside the northeastern cities of Boston, New York, and Philadelphia appeared to meet these specifications. For reasons of convenience I chose to study the Connecticut communities nearest New York City. Connecticut vested most of its regulatory powers pertaining to land use in local governments, and some of the communities in western Connecticut were part of the long-established but still expanding New York metropolitan area.[3]

The study design

Because the interested parties, the pattern of interaction between them, and the associated processes of control should be most visible when governments consider proposals to develop land, the most fruitful means for describing and explaining patterns of control would be through case histories of real estate developments in representative communities. Because a community's position in a regional economy influences the type of development proposed for it, the analysis requires, in addition to a focus on particular developments, a focus on the place of the community in the regional political economy. To achieve this dual focus, I adopted a nested research design which featured ethnographies of real estate development supplemented by analyses of the political economy of development in the surrounding community and region.

The analysis begins with a description, using aggregate data, of the most visible patterns in western Connecticut land-use conversion and control. The data come from a variety of sources. Cadastral surveys based on the tax records of 32 Connecticut communities provided measures of changes in the pattern of landholding. Skeletal histories of real estate development and its regulation could be constructed from documents in municipal archives. Census publications provided information on changes in the socio-economic composition of communities.

The setting: suburbanization in western Connecticut

The shaded portions of figure 2 indicate the region under study. It extends 90 miles from north to south and includes a wide range of community types.

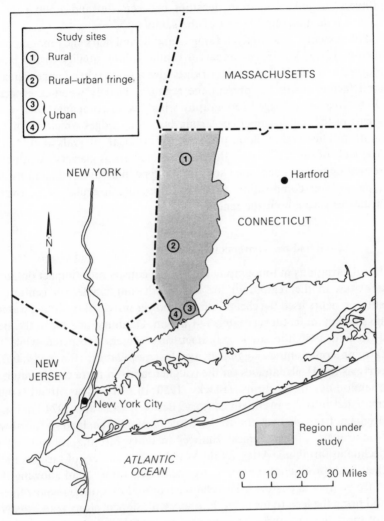

Figure 2 *The sample of communities*

At one extreme, in northwestern Connecticut, there are farming communities with large tracts of forested land, population densities of only 20 persons per square mile, and low rates of conversion from rural to urban uses. At the other extreme, in southwestern Connecticut, there are several slow-growing, built-up urban centers which have little undeveloped land, population densities of more than 3,000 persons per square mile, and low rates of land-use conversion. Rural–urban fringe communities with higher rates of land-use conversion and population densities between 100 and 1,500 persons per square mile make up the rest of the sample.

Hills extending north from Long Island Sound mark the topography of the region. Long, low ridges impart a gentle, rolling quality to the landscape along the coast; higher, rockier ridges give a more rugged appearance to the land farther north. At present the region is heavily wooded, especially in those areas with rugged topography where water companies own land. The farms in the region are either strung out along ridges which run north and south or clustered on flood plains which occur at intervals along the rivers. The soils of the region bear the marks of numerous glaciers. Advancing and retreating glaciers deposited soils of one type in areas dominated by another type, so soil composition varies in dramatic, irregular ways over short distances throughout the region.

Land-use conversion

Local variations in topography have had a considerable impact on economic activities in the region. In the eighteenth and nineteenth centuries local entrepreneurs used the cheap source of power provided by falling water to set up small manufacturing centers in Canaan, Danbury, and Norwalk. Between 1870 and 1940 the small manufacturing centers prospered while nearby farming communities stagnated and lost population (Black, 1950:73). As early as the 1860s families on the rougher lands in these communities began abandoning their farms (Black, 1950:167–71). This trend continued unabated into the twentieth century. Between 1929 and 1974 land in farms declined from 44 percent to 10 percent of all the land in northwestern Connecticut.[4] Technological changes in dairy farming contributed to the decline in farmland. After World War I large numbers of farmers increased their milk production by confining their cows rather than allowing them to graze on upland pastures. This change required that farmers mow their fields and bring the feed to the cows. Farmers with sloped, stony land usually could not mow their pastures, so they either engaged in the expensive practice of purchasing feed from off the farm or resigned themselves to lower levels of production per cow. Under these circumstances disproportionate numbers of farmers on hilly, upland sites went out of business. Beginning in the 1920s wealthy residents of New York City began purchasing these farms and farmhouses for use as summer homes. By 1934 summer homes made up approximately 15 percent of all of the homes in Fairfield and Litchfield counties (Whetten and Rapaport, 1936).

Suburban development began in earnest following World War II. It

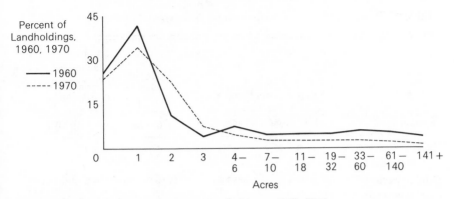

Figure 3 *The changing distribution of landholdings, 1960–1970*

produced large changes in land use, but they occurred in small, annual increments. Between 1960 and 1970, a period of rapid real estate development, developed land increased by only 5.8 percent, from 32.4 percent to 38.2 percent of all land in western Connecticut.[5] Changes in the distribution of landownership accompanied the increase in built-up land. The data in figure 3 document this change.[6] Between 1960 and 1970 development reduced the number of large, undeveloped landholdings such as farms, increased the number of homes on spacious one, two, and three acre lots and reduced the relative, if not the absolute, number of small, developed landholdings such as mobile homes on quarter acre lots.[7]

Rates of land-use conversion rose and fell as a wave of suburban development beginning in the communities closest to New York City moved through the region (see table 1). In the 1950s the communities closest to New York experienced rapid suburban development while communities farther from the city experienced a slow, but steady rate of growth. In the 1960s and 1970s growth slowed in the southwestern Connecticut communities closest to New York, remained rapid in the rural–urban fringe communities of middlewestern Connecticut, and continued at a slow, steady pace in the rural communities of northwestern Connecticut. Histories of land-use conversion in each subregion underline the circumstances which triggered the changes in rates of development.

Suburbanization began in southwestern Connecticut in the 1920s and 1930s when the creation of commuter rail service and the construction of the Merritt Parkway made daily commuting to New York City feasible for the first time (Whetten, 1942). The in-migration of affluent businessmen and their families caused moderate increases in population during the 1930s and

Table 1. *Population and land-use changes in western Connecticut*

Region	Population change (%)			Land-use change (%) (change in undeveloped land area, 1960–1970)
	1950–1960	1960–1970	1970–1980	
Northwestern Connecticut	+18.2	+17.5	+9.7	−2.7
Middlewestern Connecticut	+50.3	+57.6	+21.1	−9.8
Southwestern Connecticut	+51.7	+24.6	−2.1	−6.0

Note: The slowing rates of population growth between 1950 and 1980 for all three categories of communities reflect larger regional and national trends in rates of natural increase and population growth.
Sources: For population: Edward G. Stockwell, Town and Country Fact Book, 1960 (Storrs, Connecticut: Agricultural Experiment Station, Bulletin No. 380, 1964); Speahr, Tom, Vincent Boldae, and Catherine Skambis, Town and County Fact Book, 1970 (Storrs, Connecticut: Agricultural Experiment Station, Bulletin No. 426, 1974). 1980 Census of Population and Housing, Summary Statistics for Governmental Units and Standard Metropolitan Statistical Areas: Connecticut. For land use: tax records for northwestern and middlewestern Connecticut communities; municipal reports for southwestern Connecticut communities.

1940s (Spectorsky, 1955). Growth rates accelerated in the 1950s when developers began building large numbers of single-family homes for young families with children. Land-use conversion slowed in the 1960s when a growing scarcity of undeveloped land reduced the number of single family homes which developers could build. The decline in the supply of new homes coincided with increases in demand caused by the relocation of corporate headquarters to southwestern Connecticut. These two trends pushed the prices for single-family homes to high levels in the early 1970s.

Rates of real estate development just to the north, in middlewestern Connecticut, were high throughout the 1950s, and they rose to still higher levels in the 1960s with the completion of two interstate highways. The new highways, I-684 and I-84, made it possible to commute from homes around Danbury to workplaces in New York City and southern Westchester County. By increasing the feasible commuting distance, the completion of

Table 2. *Prices per acre for undeveloped land in middlewestern Connecticut communities (in dollars)*

Communities	Year				
	1950	1955	1960	1965	1970
North of corridor	60	235	231	336	1339
	(15)	(14)	(16)	(14)	(16)
I-84 corridor	234	427	230	355	1995
	(14)	(15)	(14)	(16)	(15)
South of corridor	485	450	519	3250	3883
	(12)	(10)	(16)	(5)	(18)

Notes: The average prices were computed from the advertised prices of all undeveloped land offered for sale in the real estate sections of local newspapers in 1950, 1955, 1960, 1965, and 1970. The figures in parentheses under the prices indicate the number of advertised land parcels that year. The small number of parcels advertised in the southern towns in 1965 increases the margin of error for that estimate.

Sources: The Danbury *News-Times*, the Newtown *Bee*, The Westport *News*, and the Lakeville *Journal*.

the new roads caused a sudden expansion in the land area available for residential real estate development. In hopes of capitalizing on the sudden increase in access to the center city, large numbers of landowners along I-84 put their land up for sale in the late 1950s. Figure 4 and table 2 indicate the effects of the increase in the supply of undeveloped land on its price in the I-84 corridor as well as immediately to the north and south of the corridor.[8,9] The 50 percent decline in the price of undeveloped land in the I-84 corridor between 1955 and 1960, just before the completion of the new road, produced the low land prices which enabled developers to build inexpensive 'starter' homes in these communities throughout the 1960s. The resulting geography of housing made for simple search strategies among young city couples intent on moving to the Connecticut suburbs. Starting in the exclusive communities along the coast, they drove north until they found something they could afford.

The rapid rates of growth together with the characteristics of the in-migrants created fiscal problems for local governments on the rural–urban fringe. The availability of starter homes attracted large numbers of families with small children. The subsequent rise in school enrollments required

Table 3. *Changes in property tax rates by region, 1959–1974*

	Average tax rates (in mills) Year		
Region	1959	1974	1959–1974 change
Rural	21.3	26.0	+4.7
Fringe	15.0	27.7	+12.7
Urban	27.0	28.6	+1.6

Interpretation: In a town with a 55.6 mill rate, a homeowner would be taxed $55.60 annually for every $1,000 of the assessed value of the house which he owns. The tax rates in the table are standardized to take into account differences between communities in the proportion of assessed property that is taxed.
Sources: Connecticut Register and Manual for Town Governments, 1959, 1974.

increases in school expenditures which could not be financed from property taxes on the starter homes. As the data in table 3 indicate, public officials frequently resolved this problem by raising taxes. Politicians also tried to raise revenue by expanding the tax base through zoning policies which promoted commercial and industrial development. When these policies succeeded, they accelerated the rate of conversion to urban land uses.

The farming communities of northwestern Connecticut felt the first impact of metropolitan expansion in the 1930s when urban residents began looking for recreational and retirement homes in these communities. For the next 40 years northwestern Connecticut communities remained outside the effective commuting range of workers in the New York metropolitan area, so land-use conversion continued at a slow rate. Only since 1975 with the completion of stretches of the new Route 7, a limited access, north–south highway (see figure 4), and the construction of large corporate headquarters in rural–urban fringe areas has it become possible for people to live in northwestern Connecticut and commute to places of work in the metropolitan area. Aware of these new possibilities, landowners in the northwestern towns anticipated an increase in the rate of real estate development in the 1980s.

The differences in growth rates between the three subregions conform roughly to the three stages of development outlined in figure 1. The rural stage, in which communities are beyond commuting range of major centers of employment and experience slow, sporadic land-use conversion, character-ized northwestern Connecticut communities between 1950 and 1980. The rural–urban fringe stage, in which communities are within commuting range

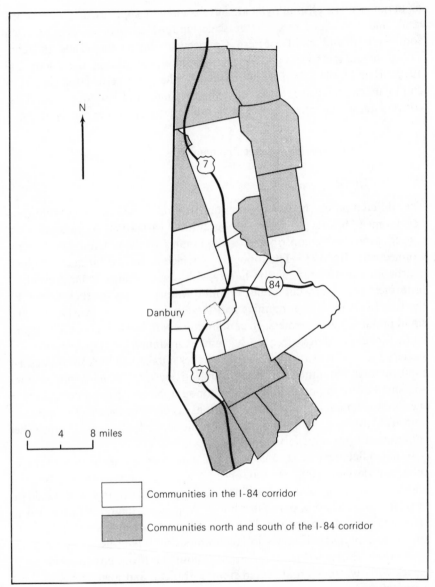

Figure 4 *Geographical boundaries in the impact of I-84 on real estate development*

of major centers of employment, have abundant supplies of undeveloped land, and experience rapid, large scale land-use conversion, characterized southwestern and middlewestern Connecticut during the 1950s and continued to characterize middlewestern Connecticut during the 1960s and 1970s. Finally, the urban stage, marked by the presence of large centers of employment, extensive tracts of built-up land, and infrequent land-use conversion, characterized southwestern Connecticut during the 1970s.

Differentiation between communities

In rural areas

The differentiation between communities which accompanies suburban development has its origins in topographical variations. As noted earlier, rugged topography contributed to high rates of farm failure in western Connecticut after 1935. The topography which distressed farmers delighted exurbanites looking for country homes with scenic settings, so large numbers of farmers in the hilly communities found willing buyers for their farms. By the late 1940s these communities had large populations of exurbanites and small populations of farmers. In communities with large tracts of flat, arable land, farms failed less frequently, and exurbanites, perhaps because the scenery was not so attractive, came in smaller numbers to look for homes. By 1950 these communities still had comparatively large farming populations and small exurban populations. These topographically derived differences in the composition of community populations account for the early adoption of land-use laws in some communities and the late adoption of laws in other communities (see appendix A).[10]

Initial differences in land-use control influenced subsequent patterns of suburban development. The presence of legal restrictions in one but not another community became a selling point for realtors trying to persuade in-migrants to purchase a particular home. Affluent in-migrants responded to arguments about the enhanced security of their investment in places with zoning and purchased homes in communities with land-use controls. Poor in-migrants responded to observations about the lower cost of housing in places without zoning and rented homes, trailers, and apartments in these communities.

These selective processes increased the economic differences between adjacent communities. As the data in table 4 suggest, the first communities to adopt land-use laws developed into affluent, residential communities while the last communities to adopt laws developed into lower income, commercial

Table 4. *Year zoned and mean family incomes: New Milford area towns*

Town	Year zoned	Mean family incomes		% change in income, 1960–1970
		1960	1970	
New Milford	1971	6073	12879	+112
Kent	1964	6298	14329	+128
Bridgewater	1959	5475	14000	+156
Washington	1938	6698	15989	+139
Roxbury	1932	6516	17341	+166

Source: Town and County Fact Books, 1960, 1970. Storrs: Agricultural Experiment Station, 1964, 1974.

centers. These trends did not go unnoticed in the latter communities. Out of exasperation mixed with apprehension a New Milford resident noted the restrictive zoning in the surrounding communities and concluded that his hometown was "a sitting duck without zoning."[11]

A note of caution: it would be a mistake to assume that all rural communities fall neatly into one or the other class of peripheral communities. In some communities, such as Litchfield, exurbanites predominate in one section of town while farmers and factory workers predominate in another section of town. In these places the onset of suburban development sparks debates over the 'character' of the community. Excerpts from a letter to the editor and an editorial response in the Litchfield *Enquirer* suggest the nature of these interchanges.

Variances in my opinion should be carefully screened and voted upon by neighboring landowners, who are made aware of the situation by mail from Town Hall, notifying them of the application with the date and time of the meeting...I am very much in favor of granting variances for creative individuals who will contribute artistic merit to our area which will add to our 'cultural' aspirations; those, however, wishing variances for commercial advancement should certainly look to other pastures because that is not what Litchfield is all about.[12]

The editor of the local newspaper, who viewed the town in a somewhat different light, could not resist responding.

Re: "creative individuals who will contribute to the artistic merit" of the area being the only approved persons, we don't feel that Litchfield is 'about' being a rural Greenwich Village...its whole history is 'about' farms and cows and horses and others of God's creatures easier to live with than many of His people.[13]

In rural–urban fringe areas

Developers' sensitivity to changes in the restrictiveness of land-use regulations in fringe areas accelerates processes of socio-economic differentiation between communities. When one community imposes a set of restrictive regulations, the affected developers shift their operations to other communities which continue to permit intense land uses. The history of apartment construction in the Danbury–New Milford region illustrates the link between the adoption of more restrictive regulations in one place and a surge of development in another place. In the late 1960s after the completion of I-84 and I-684 made it possible to commute from the Danbury area to places of work near New York City, several developers decided to build apartment complexes around Danbury. Until 1967 the zoning commission in Brookfield, a suburb of Danbury, had never received an application to build apartments; in 1968 the commission processed three applications for apartment complexes. Out of fears that apartment construction would convert Brookfield into a lower-income community, the commissioners declared a moratorium on apartment construction late in 1968. The following year, New Milford, immediately to the north of Brookfield, experienced a dramatic increase in the number of apartments proposed for construction. In 1969 the planning commission approved the construction of more apartments than had been built in the town up until 1968. In 1970 New Milford declared a moratorium on sewer construction which, because apartments require sewers, made it impossible to build more apartments in the town. Beginning in 1970, the number of apartments proposed for construction in Danbury and Bethel, just to the south of Brookfield, grew rapidly. Presumably, with nowhere else to build in the region, developers began to build on less desirable sites in the more urbanized communities of Danbury and Bethel. Figure 5 and table 5 outline the historical geography of apartment construction in the region.

Because renters and homeowners differ in economic status, decisions to prohibit apartments in one place and allow them in another place affect the socio-economic composition of local populations. The impact of these decisions may be especially large in the early stages of suburban development when the affected area has no firmly established pattern of land use. Rural areas without amenities like a lake or hazards like a flood plain do not have significant locational externalities. Under these circumstances the idiosyncracies of a land-use law or a local landowner often determine the characteristics of the first intense land use in an area. One owner may decide to establish a dump while another owner may decide to build single-family

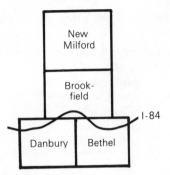

Figure 5 *Four-town map*

Table 5. *Apartment units approved by year and town*

Year	Brookfield	New Milford	Danbury	Bethel
1966	0	0	0	0
1967	0	0	5	0
1968	58	0	0	0
1969	0	500	18	0
1970	0	0	247	0
1971	0	0	134	52
1972	0	0	0	164
1973	0	0	304	87

Sources: Planning Commission Records: Bethel, Brookfield, New Milford, and Danbury.

homes. Land-use laws which arbitrarily designate one area a residential zone and another area a commercial zone produce the same result, a small subdivision of homes in one place, a race track in another place.

The first intense land use has a selective effect; it attracts some land uses and repels other land uses. Over time as land uses of a particular type accumulate in an area, a pattern with status connotations begins to emerge, and some areas become known as prestigious places to live. Prospective homeowners from the city, who spend Sunday afternoons looking at homes in fringe communities, quickly become aware of these status differences and purchase accordingly. The wealthier purchasers choose to buy in one area while the poorer purchasers buy in another area. Over time as the reputations of these places become more clearly established, the self-selection of affluent and less affluent in-migrants into different areas becomes more pronounced.

Table 6. *Residential mobility of populations in rural, rural–urban fringe, and urban communities, 1965–1970*

Region	% of town's population living in a different house than in 1965	% of those residents who moved who were living in a different state in 1965
Rural	32.8	28.9
Fringe	42.2	30.2
Suburbs and cities	42.4	49.4

Source: Town and County Fact Book, 1970.

Migration within fringe areas adds to the economic differences between local populations. Many of these moves involve 'trading up' in homes. Census data indirectly suggests the extent to which fringe area populations trade up in housing. Families in fringe communities tend to be poorer and younger than families in core communities. In 1970 the median family income was $12,681 in the fringe communities compared to $17,560 in the core communities. The median age was 28.6 years in the fringe communities compared with 31.1 years in the core communities.[14] These patterns reflect the presence of large numbers of first home purchasers in fringe area populations and imply that a large segment of these populations wants to trade up. The migration data from table 6 indicate that, while the residents of rural–urban fringe areas were just as mobile as the residents of urban areas, a larger proportion of their moves were within the local area in which they lived. If, as John Goodman (1978:15) has argued, households move short distances to improve their housing and long distances to improve their jobs, then the differences in residential mobility between rural–urban fringe and urban communities probably reflect the larger number of households in fringe areas who were trading up in housing, moving, for example, from a mobile home in New Milford to a single-family home in nearby Sherman. As trading up becomes common in a fringe area, it redistributes prosperous households away from emerging commercial centers and towards newly created suburbs. It becomes one more source for the emerging system of stratification between communities.

Table 7 describes the process of stratification in western Connecticut between 1960 and 1980. The standard deviation of the median family

Table 7. *The stratification of places in western Connecticut, 1960–1980*

1 Rural region

Median family income

	1960	1970	1980
Urban center	5628	10551	17076
Rural	6271	11151	19850
Rural	5486	11405	20208
Rural	5932	10157	18009
Rural	6255	11588	21953
St. dev. (adjusted)[a]	319	288	520

Population increase, 1960–1980 = 11.7%
Population density, 1970 = 57 persons/sq. mile

2 Rural–urban fringe region

Median family income

	1960	1970	1980
City	6584	11394	23465
Suburb	6865	12317	26608
Suburb	6926	11742	27458
Suburb	7939	16833	38476
Suburb	8011	14835	37500
Suburb	8045	14146	29943
St. dev. (adjusted)	658	1006	1360

Population increase, 1960–1980 = 94.3%
Population density, 1970 = 616 persons/sq. mile

3 Urban region

Median family income

	1960	1970	1980
City	7420	12507	25479
Suburb	11370	21435	43459
Suburb	10185	20755	44522
Suburb	12998	22171	46133
Suburb	13310	23889	49264
Suburb	12790	23626	49705
St. dev. (adjusted)	2000	2094	2159

Population increase, 1960–1980 = 22.3%
Population density, 1970 = 1321 persons/sq. mile

[a] The standard deviations have been adjusted for inflation. They are in 1960 dollars.
Sources: Town and County Fact Books, 1960, 1970; 1980 Census of Population and Housing, Summary Statistics for Governmental Units and Standard Metropolitan Statistical Areas: Connecticut.

incomes of the communities in a subregion measures the degree of stratification in a subregion. A high standard deviation indicates a high degree of stratification; an increase in the standard deviation over time indicates growth in the degree of stratification (Logan, 1976a). A comparison of the rates of population growth and stratification across the three subregions suggests that the more rapid the rate of population growth in an area, the more quickly the communities become stratified. The high degree of stratification which characterizes urban communities emerges during earlier periods of rapid land-use conversion.

As the communities in a subregion become more stratified, popular conceptions of places change. Residents of developing suburbs begin to regard their community as a "garden spot" in an expanding sea of single-family homes and shopping centers. Similarly the residents of developing commercial centers begin to describe their community in terms of its differences from the surrounding suburbs. After alluding to the exclusivity of the surrounding suburbs, the first selectman of a growing commercial center described his community as

an American town, receptive to people of all types. We have mobile parks; we have apartments; we have regular housing developments, and we have exclusive housing developments.[15]

As a region becomes more built up, these contrasting conceptions of community become well known, and, in caricatured form, they contribute to the antagonism between cities and suburbs which marks land-use politics in the metropolitan core.

Patterns of land use control

The description of land-use controls to this point has been confined to an examination of the effects which the adoption of land-use laws has on processes of differentiation between communities. The cross-sectional data assembled in table 8 reveal other patterns in western Connecticut land-use planning. The data represent an inventory of all the actions taken in 1979 by land-use authorities in four representative communities. The legal powers of the authorities are more limited in the rural community than they are in the other three communities. The rural community has no formal controls over commercial and industrial land uses. It only exercises control over subdivision requests, almost all of which concern residential developments. The other communities have zoning laws, subdivision regulations, and site plan review procedures, so all major changes in land use must be approved

Table 8. *Patterns of land-use planning in four communities, 1979*

	Rural (Goshen)	Rural–urban fringe (New Milford)	Suburb (Westport)	Satellite city (Norwalk)
Subdivision activity	44 units in 10 proposals	600 units in 27 proposals	104 units in 12 proposals	486 units in 16 proposals
Number of proposals	10	33	24	26
Out-of-town developers (% of proposals)	20%	53%	33%	26%
Commission actions (% denied)	0%	21%	63%	18%
Citizen opposition (% of proposals which generated opposition)	10%	15%	64%	43%
Court cases (% of proposals which generated court cases)	0%	5%	50%	13%

Notes: "Subdivision activity" refers to all proposals to construct housing units. "Number of development proposals" includes proposals for industrial and commercial as well as residential developments. "Out-of-town developers" include developers whose offices are located outside the community and developers who previously maintained offices outside the community and have moved their base of operations to the community within the past five years. "Commission actions" refers to the percentage of all commission actions which denied an application to build. "Citizen opposition" occurs if one or more persons objects to a development proposal at a public hearing. "Court cases" refers to the percentage of all commission actions which were appealed in the state courts. This count is based on the recollections of local land use authorities about each case.

Sources: 1979 Planning Commission Minutes, Goshen; 1979 Minutes, Planning and Zoning Commissions, New Milford, Norwalk, and Westport; interviews with land use authorities in each community.

by a legal authority. Table 8 presents data on projects, developers, land-use decisions, and the incidence of land-use conflict in each of the four communities.

Comparisons across the four communities reveal a pattern of activity which is consistent with the structural shifts in suburban development and land-use planning outlined in figure 1. The rate of development is higher and out of town developers are more common in rural–urban fringe communities than they are in rural communities. As indicated in the data on commission actions, the rural community pursues the most permissive and the suburban community the most restrictive policies. The two measures of land-use conflict, citizen opposition at public hearings and litigation following commission decisions, both indicate higher levels of conflict in urban communities than in rural or rural–urban fringe communities. The dramatic differences between the suburb and the satellite city in the number of court cases raises questions about urban land-use politics which will be addressed in the case studies.

Regional analyses and case studies of land-use planning

The changes in western Connecticut's population and land markets between 1950 and 1980 confirm the existence of the structural shifts described in chapter 2. These changes provide the starting points for more detailed examinations of how local political processes generate the patterns of control observed in table 8. This line of reasoning uses the theoretical formulations developed in chapter 2 to derive hypotheses about how overarching structural changes alter interactions between participants in land-use conversion and, in so doing, create pressure for new forms of land-use control. Two arguments, concerning transitions from rural to rural–urban fringe areas and from fringe to urban areas, make the link between structure and process. Summaries of the arguments should make clear the type of data required to evaluate them.

As rural communities evolve into rural–urban fringe areas, the ownership of land changes more often and local residents become more mobile. Because new land uses can cause dramatic changes in the value of nearby land uses, the rising rate of land-use conversion increases the prospective gains and losses to landowners; in this context they redouble their efforts to situate themselves among an optimal group of users. Homeowners interested in 'trading up' look to buy among wealthy homeowners; storeowners try to situate themselves near stores with desirable clientele, and developers respond to changes in regulations with rapid shifts to new locations. The increased rates of change in landowners and homeowners destroy recurrent relationships between neighboring landowners. In effect neighbors move from an iterated to a single play social dilemma when rural places become rural–urban fringe areas. This shift, according to the tenets of game theory, should increase the incidence of short-term, self-seeking behaviors and reduce the effectiveness of bilateral relational controls. Under these circumstances local residents should express a growing preference for rule-based controls capable of disciplining developers.

As rural–urban fringe areas evolve into urban communities, the political effects of the differentiation which accompanies development become obvious. As areas become built-up, developers try to take advantage of external economies by grouping similar land uses and separating dissimilar uses; over time this process creates clusters of property owners who make similar uses of land and share the same interests in the development of nearby tracts of land. The similarity in interests facilitates coalition formation and, indirectly, the entry of neighborhood groups into local politics. Their entry into politics increases the opposition which developers encounter in a community. As the level of conflict increases, local governments look for third parties, planners, to manage the conflicts. While conflicts occur everywhere, their substance varies according to the balance of power in the community. In developer-dominated cities shoddy construction in recently completed developments as well as proposals for new development become foci for conflict; in homeowner-controlled suburbs conflict always concerns proposals for further development.

Both of the arguments which link structures and processes involve extrapolations from aggregate data. The extrapolations may be reasonable, but they are speculative, and, as such, they reveal the limitations of the preceding analysis. Information about crucial processes is lacking. Arguments about the effects of changes in social relations on informal land-use controls or the effects of changes in the incidence of conflict on the role of planners can not be assessed with aggregate data. Case studies can provide these data. From interviews with landowners and archival research one can construct detailed historical accounts of land-use planning and interactions between interested parties which will either confirm or disconfirm arguments which link the two phenomena. The interviews provide composite accounts of the interactions surrounding four or five development projects in each community. A formal test of these arguments would require more systematic sampling of a larger number of development projects in each area than I have been able to carry out. This limitation notwithstanding, the data from the case studies do provide a wealth of empirical materials which illustrate the potential of this explanatory approach. The field methods employed in gathering the case study materials are outlined below.

Case study methods

Field research took place over a period of eight years, from 1974 to 1982. A continuous period of field research from the fall of 1974 until the summer of 1975 was followed by summers of field research in 1977, 1978, 1981, and 1982. The research involved the collection of ethnographic data on real estate development in four places in western Connecticut. The numbers 1, 2, 3 and 4 in figure 2 indicate the location of these places. The research in each place focused on the land use histories of particular neighborhoods. The chief source of information for the histories was provided by 120 semi-structured interviews, 30 in each neighborhood. In each interview a homeowner or landowner was asked questions about land-use problems and the history of real estate development in the neighborhood. The interviews averaged about 75 minutes in length. Because some respondents had lived in the neighborhood much longer than other respondents, they had more stories to tell, and these interviews took as long as two and one-half hours to complete.[16]

The most useful information in the interviews came from the stories. Because the argument presented in chapter 2 focuses on changes in social relations among interested landowners, the interview data on the respondent's relations with neighbors, developers, and land-use officials had the most direct bearing on the arguments under examination. The relational data came out in the respondents' accounts of the events surrounding land-use changes in their neighborhoods. To insure that I gathered a representative sample of the real estate development stories in a neighborhood, I drew a random sample of landowners in an area. Further details on the sampling strategy, the response rate, and the interview schedule are presented in appendix B.

To understand the historical and political context within which developments occurred, I collected additional interview and archival data in each community. To improve my understanding of the contemporary political context, I conducted approximately 20 open-ended interviews with local notables in real estate development. The identity of these individuals varied from community to community, but they usually included a prominent developer, a planning and zoning commissioner, the town planner, and the reporter who covered planning and zoning affairs for the local newspaper. To add to this record of interview data, I read extensively in the back issues of the newspapers which reported on planning and zoning. To gauge how land-use conversion and control had evolved in each community, I read all of the planning and zoning items in the local newspaper for selected periods of time. For the satellite city, Norwalk, I read all of the planning and zoning items in the late 1930s when the community was beginning to feel the initial pressures of suburbanization. I repeated the procedure for the 1954–1955 period when Norwalk was experiencing rapid suburbanization, and again for the 1976–1982 period when real estate development was occurring more slowly. I did the same type of archival work in the three other communities.

The municipal archives also contained valuable documents. Court reporters' transcripts of contentious town meetings proved especially useful. The minutes of planning and zoning commission meetings varied widely in quality, but occasionally they offered illuminating insights into the pattern of local control. Countless conversations with town clerks (who know everything!) and interested bystanders helped me fill in the remaining gaps in the local real estate development story. On five occasions involving particularly controversial proposals for development, I attended the public hearings on the development.

To place the pattern of land-use control observed in the four communities in a regional perspective, I carried out 82 additional interviews with prominent actors in the land development and planning process in western Connecticut. I chose the respondents on the recommendations of local public officials who described them as especially knowledgeable about planning and zoning in the region. Of the persons approached for interviews, only four, all developers, refused to be interviewed. The interests of the informants varied widely. The persons interviewed included regional planners, specialists in soil conservation, citizen activists in attempts to block the construction of an interstate highway, and developers who built in several different communities in the region. On a number of occasions, especially while conducting research in rural northwestern Connecticut, I sought out information on land-use control in nearby communities. These data provided a comparative perspective on patterns of land-use control in the case study community.

Several facets of the study may convey an overly ordered conception of the research process. The research methods, which ranged from the participant observation and unstructured interview techniques favored by ethnographers to the secondary data analyses used by demographers, may have been particularly appropriate for the study of a phenomenon in which individual landowners, local politicians, and the metropolitan land economy all figure prominently, but this mix of methods was not predetermined. Rather the research strategy employed was *ad hoc* and sequential in character. The research began with materials on file in town halls, moved on to interviews with local notables in real estate development, and concluded with the ethnographic studies of real estate development. This untidy, but persistent program of research generated the findings reported in the following chapters.

4 A rural community

Introduction

In 1980 the population of Goshen exceeded 1,700 persons for the first time since the middle of the nineteenth century. Like other northwestern Connecticut communities, Goshen experienced a prolonged period of out-migration beginning in the 1860s, when farmers with sheep and cattle, faced with competition from western ranchers, abandoned their small hillside farms. In the early twentieth century dairy farming became the dominant agricultural activity in the community. It remains so today. Beginning in the 1930s, a small stream of migrants from the New York metropolitan area began to settle in the community. Although the population and the economy have changed considerably in the twentieth century, the government retains its nineteenth-century form. A town clerk and a first selectman administer the day to day affairs of local government. Important decisions, such as the abolition of land-use controls or the adoption of the annual budget, are debated and decided upon in meetings open to all residents. In its demography, economy, and politics the town resembles other communities in northwestern Connecticut.

Land use in Goshen follows a familiar pattern. Human activities outside the town center cluster around farmhouses strung out along country roads. Woodlots, fields, and thick underbrush along boundaries separate most activities from one another. Long distances muffle sounds, and open spaces carry away smells, so intense land uses often have little impact on nearby landowners. Even in places like the commercial center where conflicting land uses are in close proximity, the small scale of most operations limits the severity of the disturbances. In this context laws which regulate land use seem superfluous, and communities usually do not have them.

Relational controls over land use

When disturbances occur, landowners in rural communities have several non-legal means of remedying the situation. Some landowners create buffer zones between their activities and the source of the disturbance. For example, an ex-farmer found the noise from passing cars so disturbing that, when he built his retirement home, he set it back several hundred feet from the road. Other landowners buffer themselves by purchasing nearby tracts of land. In 1967 a farmer put up 2,000 acres for sale in Norfolk and found a ready buyer in a developer from Hartford. The land for sale contained a large stretch of forested land with a few open fields and a bog. When the news circulated about town that the prospective buyer wanted to put a large subdivision of single-family homes on the land, local conservationists put their heads together and came up with a two-point plan of action. The Nature Conservancy agreed to purchase the bog, and a prominent Norfolk family outbid the developer for 700 acres of woodland. To ease their financial burden, the family subdivided the purchased acreage among themselves and sold several tracts of land to friends who promised not to develop it. With the reduced amount of land available for development, the developer cancelled his plans to purchase the farm (Childs, 1975).

Environmental protection through the creation of buffer zones requires inexpensive land. Even then the purchase of adjoining lands is only an option for wealthy residents, and more specifically, for wealthy residents who, like the Norfolk conservationists, can mobilize other members of their families for concerted action. Poor residents usually do not have the financial resources to purchase a home, much less a buffer zone around a home. When suburban development increases the price of undeveloped land, its purchase for use as a buffer zone becomes prohibitively expensive, even for wealthy landowners.

The residents of rural communities also rely on informal social controls to regulate land use.[1] In some cases they exercise control through complaints. The homeowners in lakeshore cottages across the street from a lumber yard in Morris exercised control through complaints. The owner of the lumber yard, an elderly woman, Mrs. Harrison, lived in a home next to the lumber yard. She and her lakefront neighbors visited one another frequently, and, if activities at the lumber yard began to bother the neighbors, they would mention it to Mrs. Harrison on one of their visits. Because Mrs. Harrison wanted to maintain amicable relations with her neighbors and did not have a burning desire to increase her income in her declining years, she heeded her neighbors' requests and kept her lumber operations unobtrusive and small in

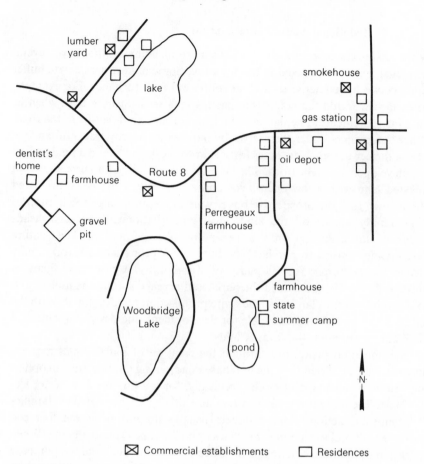

Figure 6 *Goshen, mid 1970s*

scale. In other cases the developer solicits the advice of his neighbors. Before Phillip Nadeau built a smokehouse behind his home on Main Street in Goshen (see figure 6), he consulted with all of his neighbors.[2] In this case, as in the case of the lumber yard, the opinions of the neighboring landowners operated as an informal control over commercial land use in a neighborhood.

These relational controls over land use assume that neighbors have a considerable regard for one another, that they listen to and act on one another's complaints. The Citizen's Committee for an Unzoned Norfolk made this assumption explicit in a flyer distributed just before a referendum on the adoption of zoning in Norfolk. They argued that the townspeople are an above average group in both intelligence and in willingness to accept their moral obligations to their neighbors. They do not need to be compelled to build adequate houses and building establishments.[3]

The pattern of real estate development which prevails in rural communities makes relational controls particularly effective. A large number of homes are constructed one at a time on lands belonging to local farmers. In many instances the occupants of the new homes are relatives of the farmer: children who continue to farm build homes on land near the original farmhouse. Even children who leave farming sometimes build nearby. On one occasion the son of a Goshen farmer worked off the farm, but he built his house on a lot which his parents had subdivided from the farm and given to him as a wedding present. Over time this pattern of real estate development creates a residential pattern in which many neighbors are relatives. The kin ties between neighbors facilitate communication and give individuals leverage in discussions about the location of a small dump or the disposal of rusting machinery.

In other cases the farmer sells the new homes to strangers. Frequently age has forced a farmer to reduce the scale of his agricultural operations. In this circumstance the periodic sale of land or a house provides the farmer with a valuable increment to his income. Sons or other relatives of the farmer build the homes on lots which the farmer has subdivided from the rest of his lands. To avoid the expense of constructing an access road, the farmer usually builds the new homes on lots which front on a road. Because the farmer's home usually fronts on the same road, his home and the new homes are often on adjacent plots of land. The three homes immediately to the north of the Perregeaux farmhouse in figure 6 illustrate this situation. These homes were built in the 1960s on lands subdivided from Ray Perregeaux's farm. Because Mr. Perregeaux continues to live within sight of the homes which he constructs, he has an incentive to build houses which are not an eyesore and do not contain structural defects which would cause the new owners to complain to the builder.[4] The shadow of the farmer–developer's future relations with the homeowners encourages him to exercise self-control in the construction of homes. This set of circumstances characterizes most development projects in Goshen. Of the ten land-use conversions proposed in 1979, eight came from local residents who wanted to carve new building lots out of larger landholdings which contained their homes.[5]

The pattern of advice and consent which preceded the construction of offices for Mickey Butkowski's oil and gas business offers some insight into the limitations of relational controls over land use. Most Goshen residents in the 1960s regarded Mickey as one of the town 'fathers'. For three decades he had owned and operated one of the two gas stations in the town, and in that capacity he had, at various times, for various reasons, extended credit for the purchase of gasoline to almost everyone in town. This practice had placed most people figuratively, if not literally, in his debt. Mickey's good works extended to local government where over a 30-year period he had served on innumerable town commissions. In the late 1960s he wanted to construct an office for his oil and gas business on lands adjoining several single-family homes. Mickey knew each of the homeowners, and, before he broke ground on the new building, he visited each of them to inform them of his plans. Although the operation of the oil and gas business promised to create occasional nuisances for the homeowners, no one objected to the development. Even after it came out that Mickey planned to operate a used-car business out of the rear of the building, none of the homeowners objected to the new land use. They did not want to jeopardize their friendship with Mickey by complaining about the impact of his business on their homes.[6] The shadow of the neighbors' future relations with Butkowski induced cooperative responses when their interests in land might have dictated otherwise.

This example suggests that under a system of bilateral relational controls, influential landowners rarely face any constraints in deciding how to use their land. Neighbors complain to receptive or politically weak landowners like Mrs. Harrison, but they do not complain to powerful, profit-minded landowners like Mickey Butkowski. Politically prominent landowners not only feel less social pressure than other landowners, they apply it to greater effect. What is more, if they cannot persuade a neighboring land user to change his plans for real estate development, influential landowners often have the financial resources necessary to purchase the land for use as a buffer zone. In the absence of formal controls the rich and powerful enjoy special advantages in shaping the use of land.

The changing community of interests in land

The faith which rural residents place in relational controls rests on an appreciation of trends in land use, relations with neighbors, and the values which people place in land. When in-migration from a nearby metropolitan area begins, the empirical bases for these beliefs begins to erode, and residents begin to question the efficacy of relational controls over land use.

The influx of exurbanites causes small, unobtrusive changes in neighborhood activities which, by changing relations between neighbors, make it more difficult for them to arrive at informal agreements about land use. The oldtimers in Goshen adjusted to the presence of strangers in the community by becoming more private in their ways. An old man who used to walk his dog along a country road, exchanging salutations with passing motorists, gradually became unsettled by the increasing number of strange faces in passing cars, so he took to walking his dog in the woods behind his house. Longtime residents, who used to sit on their front porches and watch the passing cars on summer evenings, noted the same change in motorists and moved their chairs around to the backyard where they were free from the scrutiny of strangers.

The casual uses which Goshen residents made of one another's land also changed. Sometimes growing out of mutual aid arrangements and sometimes out of long acquaintance, most Goshen residents had informal agreements permitting them to ski, hunt, fish, and snowmobile on one another's land. With these agreements young men could lay a 20-mile snowmobile tract across private lands without fear of trespassing. These arrangements disintegrated when exurbanites began erecting no trespassing signs on their land or restricting winter use of their lands to cross country skiing.[7] The residential associations in the new developments furthered this process by requiring a fee for the use of lands or water within their boundaries. For some of the poorer residents of Goshen the fees meant a sudden loss of recreational lands. One old man remarked on this change with some bitterness.

Now you got to be a member; you got to own property. If you don't pay dues, you don't benefit at all. You can't go fishing or swimming at all.[8]

On occasion the influx of newcomers produced changes in the attitudes of longtime Goshen residents towards trespassing. For instance, after the state opened up a camp for city children on lands adjacent to a Goshen farm, children from the camp began to make unauthorized use of the forests and fields on the farm, and the farmer responded by posting his land with no trespassing signs. With this exception, most longtime Goshen residents did not post their lands and resented the no trespassing signs erected by newcomers. These changes in casual land uses increased the social distance between neighbors and, in so doing, reduced the likelihood that concern over continued good relations with neighbors would induce landowners to compromise with one another when they disagree about land uses.

The disagreements between neighbors occur frequently when one landowner is an oldtimer and the other landowner is a newcomer to the community. Newcomers and oldtimers usually disagree in their estimates of the effects of a land-use change. For example, when a developer announced plans to build a small marina on a lake in Washington, Connecticut, exurbanites with lakeshore cottages expressed fears that the construction of the marina would increase boat traffic on the lake and initiate a process of commercial real estate development along the lakeshore. The longtime residents of Washington disagreed, arguing that, because the projected marina would be small in size and far from nearby houses, it would not increase boating traffic or begin a process of commercial development along the lakeshore. In other instances longtime residents came to similar conclusions. Several Goshen residents assumed that the Woodridge Lake development would never get off the ground.[9] The initial reaction of the Bantam Board of Burgesses to a proposal to build a low-income apartment complex shows traces of the same attitude. One burgess described the board's usual work.

The biggest issues we've had to deal with are whether or not to put two streetlights or three on Cathole Road, and even then we would debate a half hour.[10]

In this context the Board of Burgesses considered an application to build 168 units of subsidized housing.

At first, in December 1980, the subsidized housing seemed no more unsettling than street lights. Mr. Riva and Mr. Carr, who had collaborated on low income developments in Canaan and Meriden, presented their proposal to the Borough Board and 25 listeners and asked for approval of their concept for the Carriage Park development. No one strenuously objected...and the board granted approval.

Frankly, Mr. [Kent] Gilyard said, the board figured nothing would be heard from the men again. "For almost a year we heard nothing from nobody" added Randall Richardson, the warden, "and all of a sudden they came back and said they were ready to build."[11]

In each instance the longtime residents, accustomed to small scale, isolated land-use changes, minimized the probability of extensive changes in land use. The belief that land-use changes occur infrequently and involve only small, inexpensive tracts of land would incline someone towards reliance on bilateral relational controls over land use. When land-use changes occur infrequently, the neighbors are more likely to make a special effort to dissuade a local landowner from going ahead with a change in land use. When the land-use conversion involves a small parcel and promises small economic gains, special efforts by friends and neighbors might cause a landowner to abandon his plans for change. The wave of land-use conversions which coincides with the incorporation of a community into a metropolitan area overwhelms these efforts. These conversions involve large tracts of land and large sums of money, so potential developers are likely to turn a deaf ear to conservationist appeals from nearby landowners. The neighbors are also unlikely to voice an appeal. The prospect of large profits and a move elsewhere undermines their willingness to defend the prevailing pattern of land use in an area. Exurbanites, accustomed to the interconnectedness of land-use changes in metropolitan areas, are quick to see waves of development and, when they do, they are more likely to scoff at claims for the effectiveness of informal controls over land use.

In addition to differences in their visions of the future, newcomers and oldtimers differ in the value which they attach to particular land uses. For instance, in the late 1940s one of the first exurbanites to move to a northwestern Connecticut community decided to build a house on a ridge overlooking the town center. When a long-time resident heard about the location of the new home, he remarked that "you can't live on a view." He would have preferred a location in the town center where almost every building had some commercial potential. In another case an exurbanite owned a home located on the same road as a 'working' farm. The farm had an assemblage of junked cars and rusting farm machinery strewn about a side yard close to the road. The farmer had learned to live with his junkyard in part because he was 'mining' the machinery for spare parts. The exurbanite, in contrast, found the machinery so unsightly that he spoke with the town's building inspector in an attempt to get it moved. These examples suggest that status concerns affect the definition of a disturbance. For an exurbanite who purchased a particular home for its rustic, country setting, the sight of single-family homes under construction causes alarm. For a long-time resident, with less interest in the status implications of a 'country' home, only a disruptive activity like gravel mining causes concern. Of all the landowners in a rural community, exurbanites define disturbances the most broadly.

Differences in attitudes toward the land underlie the differences in aesthetic appreciation. The following observation by an exurbanite captures the farmer's attitude toward his land (Morath and Miller, 1977: 140).

I had the feeling, as with his brother, that the land and the house, and the barns were all little more than a work place, and outmoded at that. We might as well have been wandering about in some old factory from which he had managed to escape.

For farmers the countryside is first of all a place of work, a place to make a living. Because they rely on the land for their income, farmers want the land to be at their disposal for whatever use they want to make of it; in this perspective land is a private good, and land-use laws, which curtail the right of the landowner to use his land as he pleases, draw criticism from farmers. For exurbanites, most of whom do not rely on land for their income, the countryside is first of all a park, a place valued largely for its amenities.[12] Because exurbanites usually own houses on small tracts of land surrounded by larger tracts of woodland and pasture, the preservation of the park requires that a majority of the landowners "as far as the eye can see" refrain from developing their lands. In this perspective, land is a public good. Only the creation of publicly approved constraints on individual land users, usually in the form of zoning laws, can assure the preservation of the public good.

Additional differences in interests divide exurbanites and farmers. Exurbanites, who own a single-family home on a building lot, have less flexibility in responding to disturbances than do farmers. For example, farmers and homeowners whose lands border on a small shopping center differ in the way in which they can respond to the noise generated by traffic around the stores. In the farmer's case the noise from the stores may disturb the cattle in a nearby pasture to the point where their milk production declines. In this case the farmer may choose to switch the cattle to other pastures and grow hay on the fields closest to the stores, or, if he thinks in long-range terms, he may decide to create a buffer zone between his house and the commercial area by reforesting the land. The homeowner has less flexibility because he has sunk capital into developing his property solely for use as a residence. If disturbances from the stores make it impossible to live there, the homeowner must make a costly readjustment, such as renovating the building for some other use. In general the more intense a land use, the more specialized it will be, and the less flexibility the landowner will have in responding to disturbances.

Given these differences in outlook and interests, the exurbanites' purchase of new homes and former farmhouses in close proximity to operating farms sets the stage for debates about local land-use control. The differences in aesthetic standards, assessments of trends in land use, and abilities to adjust to land-use changes reduce the likelihood that neighbors will agree about the desirability of a land use. The change in relations between neighbors reduces their leverage with one another, so, when disagreements occur, they have fewer incentives to compromise. Under these circumstances the efficacy of relational controls over land use declines, and town residents become embroiled in sometimes heated discussions about alternative forms of land-use control.

Conversion and the adoption of rule-based controls

The differences between exurbanites and farmers in their attitudes toward land and land-use controls were sharply drawn in a 1967 town meeting. An elderly farmer, Mr. Harold Vaill, opened the meeting with a long statement about the problems with zoning.

It is costing different individuals money the way we are zoned today, and it's hurting individuals in this town. (For example) developers and farmers are classified in the same way, but Mr. Kennditer on North Street is not a developer just because he sold two or three building lots...C. Angelovitch has a repair shop; L. Arofett had a baking business, Schofield had his hay business, six businesses on a two mile stretch of road and the commission still zoned it residential. Same thing happened to Carlin's business.

Then Colby had trouble with his gravel bank; we need that gravel pit in Goshen; it is the only one in town. This kid is a native, served in the Army, and is doing an essential business, and yet he is in trouble. Frederick Dreyer built a house on a lot that really wasn't a building lot because the zoning board told him to.

To this litany of individual misfortune, an exurbanite, Mrs. Jane Woods, responded,

Mr. Vaill made us a very good plea by representing and giving us biographical sketches and talking about personalities, but we are not here to be concerned with one person, me, you, or anyone. We are here to do what is best for Goshen.

To which, Mr. Elbert Howe, a retired farmer, retorted

Who is the Town of Goshen but people? All of us are people and every single one of us is important. This is the only reason I got involved in this zoning thing.

Then the chairman of the zoning commission spoke up.

We're impartial; we did what we felt would be best for the town.[13]

The differential economic impact of a land-use law explains some of these differences of opinion. Residents who own no property, a small commercial property, or a large tract of undeveloped land stand to lose from the passage of a land-use law. By prohibiting the construction of small houses on small lots, the law forces developers to build larger, more expensive houses. Over time this pattern of building alters the size distribution of homes in the community; small houses become relatively rarer, and in response to the change in their availability, the prices of small homes rise disproportionately. Because renters do not have the financial resources to purchase the larger homes, the law, by inducing price increases in the smaller homes, makes it more difficult for renters to purchase a home. By establishing minimum lot

Table 9. *Individual characteristics and political alignments on land-use controls in Goshen*

	Individual landholdings, proportion who own:			Place of work: proportion who work in the community	Mean length of residence of the family in the community (in years)
	0 acres	1–4 acres	5+ acres		
Opposed to zoning	7%	49%	44%	46%	73
Favorable to zoning	0%	70%	30%	30%	11

Note: The differences between the group means are significant at the 0.05 level for each of the three variables. A discriminant analysis, using these three variables, produces a discriminant function which correctly predicts an individual's attitude towards land-use controls in 68 percent of the cases under conditions in which random predictions would produce a 50 percent success rate. The discriminant function is significant at the 0.01 level.

Data Sources: place of work data came from city directories, landholdings data came from municipal tax records, length of residence data came from a combination of municipal voting and land records. The petitions indicating the political alignments of particular individuals are on file in the Goshen Town Hall.

area requirements, the law prevents the owners of small building lots from developing their land. By declaring small businesses in residential zones to be non-conforming uses, the law makes it difficult for the owners to obtain permission to expand their businesses. By limiting the number of building lots which a developer can put on a tract of land, the law reduces the price which developers will pay for large tracts of undeveloped land.

The differences in interests influence political alignments on issues of land-use control. A comparison, reported in table 9, of the socio-economic characteristics of Goshen residents, who signed petitions supporting or opposing the repeal of zoning in 1967, indicates that the pro-zoners tended to be newcomers who worked outside the community and owned a house on a small plot of land while the anti-zoners tended to be natives who worked in the community and owned either a large tract of land or no land at all.

The outcome of controversies between exurbanites and farmers depends on the balance of power between the two groups. As the events surrounding the repeal of zoning illustrate, differences in the internal organization of the two factions influence the outcome of struggles between them. The movement to repeal the law began with a dispute over the use of a gravel pit located on the lands of a prominent farmer in West Goshen (see figure 6). At the time of the dispute Peter Colby, a young man raised in the town and married to the daughter of another farmer, operated the gravel business and employed the prominent farmer's son as a hired hand. In the late 1950s a dentist from New York City took up residence in one of the nearby homes. He found the dust and noise generated by the passing trucks bothersome, and, in search of relief, he asked the zoning commission to place curbs on the operating hours of the gravel pit. The prospect of limits on his operation stirred Colby to action. He wrote and, with the aid of his friends, circulated a petition calling for a special town meeting to consider the repeal of Goshen's land-use law. Within two days the gravel pit operator had collected 260 signatures, far more than necessary to call the meeting. The petition signers turned out for the meeting in large numbers, and the town voted to abolish its zoning law.

Colby's kinship ties explain the ease with which he overturned the existing law. As one farmer put it, "one of the things that newcomers don't realize is that about half of the people in the town are related to one another."[14] At the center of these kinship networks are several farming families which, in the case of Goshen, have been farming in the town since the Revolutionary War. Through his business ties to one farmer and his marriage to the daughter of another farmer, Colby found himself at the center of one such kin network. A vital concern with land-use controls, coupled with an ability to mobilize an extensive kin network, explains how Colby in this instance and small groups of farmers in other instances wield so much power in deliberations over land-use controls in peripheral communities. The social connections which enable farmers to make effective use of relational controls also give them the political power to prevent the adoption of rule-based controls.

On two occasions in the ten years following the repeal of zoning, the town of Goshen held referenda on zoning, and on each occasion the voters rejected it by a narrower margin. The last time the voters considered the adoption of a land-use law, the anti-zoners prevailed by only two votes. A number of citizens now believe that "zoning is inevitable." Two trends in the local land economy inform this belief. First, the continued out-migration of farmers and in-migration of a single-family homeowners induces a shift in the distribution of landholdings toward a preponderance of landowners with houses which sit on one and two acre tracts of land. As the data in table 9 indicate, these landowners favor the adoption of land-use controls. Eventually, with continued in-migration, their political power will grow, and they will vote in land-use controls. Secondly, the type of development has begun to change. In the early 1970s seven farmers in the southern region of the town pooled about 500 acres of their land, flooded the bottom land to create Woodbridge Lake (see figure 6), and began subdividing the newly created lakeshore into building lots for single-family homes. Two of the subdivisions proposed in 1979 came from out of town developers, and both of them involved large numbers of houses, 18 in one case, ten in the other case.[15] These projects represent a dramatic increase in the scale of development, and they present local residents with a dilemma. While many Goshen residents object to the curbs imposed by land-use laws, they do not always endorse proposals for large-scale developments. The size of the projects and the reputations of the developers worry the 'natives'. Because large projects promise to transform small towns into suburbs almost overnight, longtime residents worry about disruptions which rapid, far-reaching changes might bring. They also worry about the quality of the construction in the new developments. Because the builders usually come from outside the community, long-time residents know little about the developers' previous work, and they suspect that the developers, whose next project may take them far from Goshen, do not care about establishing a local reputation for high-quality work.[16] As long as the real estate developments proposed for the town are on the scale of Mickey Butkowski's new oil and gas buildings, longtime residents vote against land-use laws, but, as the scale of proposed projects increases, their votes often go the other way, and the community moves closer to adopting a land-use law. When adoption occurs, it often takes place in an atmosphere of crisis. The community hastily adopts a land-use plan designed to prohibit a specific development; the developer, alleging some impropriety, takes the town to court, wins his case, and builds on the land. In an almost incidental way the town obtains a land-use law.

Implementing the law

Once enacted, the new laws prove difficult to implement. The problems with implementation usually begin with the writing of the law. As one Goshen resident recalled,

the zoners did not come around to us to see how we wanted to be zoned. Instead they hired an out of town firm from Simsbury to come to town and establish zoning.[17]

The planning consultants, accustomed to working for suburban municipalities, produced regulations which did not address the special problems of land-use regulation in Goshen. In both Goshen and Norfolk the planners created regulations which drew distinctions between urban uses such as light and heavy industrial production. In locales in which little land had been committed to urban uses, these regulations seemed overly specific to voters. In effect the planners had taken "city planning to the country."[18] In 1968 "overly specific regulations killed zoning" in Norfolk.[19] After the defeat a group of Norfolk exurbanites set about revising the proposed regulations. After several years of work they produced a set of regulations so simple and general that they "could have been written on the back of an envelope."[20] In 1973 Norfolk voters approved a zoning law based on the new regulations.

The new laws proved especially cumbersome in regulating small real estate developments. When the planning consultants drew up a zoning law for Goshen in the early 1960s, they designated a two-mile stretch of highway containing five stores a residential zone on the premise that the stores were too small to create disturbances for the nearby homeowners. The stores became non-conforming uses, a circumstance which required the owners to obtain permission from the Zoning Board of Appeals whenever they wanted to alter the physical layout of their businesses. To businessmen who had been told that their stores were too small to generate nuisances for their neighbors, this permit process seemed unnecessary.[21]

The incremental fashion in which small businesses expand and individuals build homes also makes for cumbersome regulatory procedures. In the early 1970s Mr. Cass, a working-class resident of Morris, decided to build a retirement home by hand. Because he worked full-time in a factory, he could only work part-time on the house. One year he installed the septic system; the next year he laid the foundations for the house, and during the third year he built the house itself. Because the law required the construction of the building within 12 months of the building permit's date of issue, Mr. Cass had to go back to the zoning commission each year to get a permit to work on the house.[22]

In the mid 1960s a similar problem arose in Kent where the newly created zoning commission objected to the practice, common among local farmers, of subdividing and selling one building lot a year. The farmers preferred to subdivide one lot at a time because (1) they wanted a supplement to their farm income, (2) they did not know whether or not they wanted to subdivide all of their land, and (3) they wanted to avoid the costs of planning a large subdivision. The commissioners wanted each farmer to subdivide all of his land at one time so they could assess the farmer's overall plan for development. After the commission wrote this requirement into law, the farmers refused to subdivide any land for six years.[23]

The limited impact of small developments on neighboring land users and the shaky political status of rural zoning commissions inclines commissioners toward lenient treatment of applicants proposing small changes in land use. In some communities applicants receive variances and rezonings on demand. Over a period of years this practice creates a pattern of spot zoning in which the boundaries of zones and the boundaries of individual properties coincide. When the commissioners practice spot zoning, they do not exert any control over land use.

When commissions reject proposals for development, allegations about the 'personal' element in decision making often follow. In rendering decisions on variances, rezonings, and subdivision applications, commissioners should, according to the law, set aside their personal feelings toward the applicant and rule on the application in light of the public's interest in promoting a harmonious pattern of land use. In low-density communities where interferences between adjacent land users are the exception rather than the rule, citizens find it difficult to perceive the public interest in prohibiting a particular land use. In this circumstance applicants assume that the enforcement of the law should be relaxed, and, as the following interchange illustrates, the commissioners sometimes disagree.

Mrs. Boden asked why the commission could not help Mr. Elton Skilton out. The secretary pointed out that the zoning regulations are not designed specifically to help any one person but (to help) the community as a whole.[24]

If a commission's decision to deny approval is difficult to understand in terms of the public interest, it is often easy to understand in terms of the applicants' and the commissioners' personal interests. In other words one person has his application approved because he is influential and has friends on the commission while another person has his application rejected because he does not get along well with a particular commissioner.

The geography of rural land use encourages this interpretation of commission decisions. For instance, in Roxbury the owner of a feedstore believes that his neighbor across the street, an airline pilot, joined the zoning commission in order to force the closing of the feedstore through a zoning commission ruling. This idea seems plausible to the feedstore owner only because, if the airline pilot had any personal complaints about land use in his neighborhood, they would have to involve the feedstore owner because he and the airline pilot are the only intense land users in that stretch of the Shepaug River valley. Because the airline pilot and the feedstore owner have disagreed in the past over issues of land use, the feedstore owner fears that he will not receive fair treatment at the hands of the zoning commission.[25] The feedstore owner is not alone in his fears. In Goshen a longtime planning commissioner wanted to resign his position in the late 1970s, but out of concern over the impartiality of his probable successor, he did not quit. As the commissioner put it,

everyone has an axe to grind. They want to get on the commission in order to keep their neighbors from doing this or that.[26]

These problems of fairness are especially acute in small towns. Because "everyone knows everyone else," most applicants are not strangers to the commissioners, and presumably in the course of long association the commissioners have formed personal opinions about most applicants. Under these conditions the commissioners have to exercise self-restraint in order to remain impartial. Not surprisingly, concern over the character of the commissioners colors evaluations of land-use planning.

it wouldn't be too bad if you could always be sure that the right five people would be on the board.[27]

A same zone plan would include a limited number of restrictions, all of which could be readily comprehended by a boob. Such a board, would, I believe, receive enthusiastic support so long as it is administered by a Board of Solomons! Good luck![28]

So, in a context where the public interest is difficult to discern and long-standing antagonisms between individuals do exist, applicants whose proposals have been denied often attribute the denial to "bad blood" between themselves and the commissioners rather than to the commissioners' interpretation of the public interest. If the rejection rankles enough, applicants mount campaigns to have the commission abolished or the commissioners recalled. In 1963 just such a campaign forced the resignation of the entire zoning commission in Morris. In announcing their resignations, the commissioners acknowledged the personal element.

There is, in the opinion of the commission and the Board, more than a mere semblance of evidence that the move against the zoning ordinance is in reality a move against certain members of the zoning authorities.[29]

The impetus behind the movement to abolish zoning in Goshen was similar. In the words of one of the organizers "we weren't against the idea of zoning; it was a more personal thing."[30]

In an atmosphere in which most builders seek exemption from the law and disappointed applicants single out commissioners for personal attacks, the administration of a land-use law would appear to be a thankless task; only the prospect of shaping the content of the community's first land-use law attracts people to the job. Environmentalists want to become commissioners in order to create protective laws, and developers want to become commissioners in order to create permissive laws. When they do become commissioners, both developers and environmentalists face conflicts of interest.

Developers often become members of a commission at their own request or at the request of residents who regard developers as experts on questions of land-use conversion. In this position developers face numerous conflicts of interest. For example, in the early 1960s the chairman of the planning commission in Goshen, who was also a farmer, made extensive use of a provision in the subdivision regulations which permitted him to detach a building lot from his property without going to the expense of preparing a plan for his subdivision. At frequent intervals he began giving notice to the other commissioners that he had subdivided another lot from his property. In this fashion the commissioner planned to build a large subdivision of single family homes without complying with costly health, fire district, and planning regulations. He used his detailed knowledge of the law to engage in a practice which violated the intent if not the letter of the law.[31]

Because environmentally concerned commissioners focus on the preservation of a collective good rather than the capture of a private good, they do not face as many conflicts of interest as developers who serve on commissions. Environmentalists are not, however, entirely free from these problems. In one community a young exurbanite, who pushed for the passage of the first zoning law and became the first chairperson of the planning and zoning commission, later joined a group of realtors who specialized in the sale of land in bucolic settings. In this capacity the exurbanite faced a conflict of interest whenever she had to rule on developments whose construction would impair the "country setting" of land which she was trying to sell.[32] Conflicts of interest like this one, which originate in a commissioner's occupation, are common in rural communities because, with large proportions of the population employed in agriculture or real estate development, it is almost inevitable that several commissioners will be drawn from occupations which routinely generate conflicts of interest for them.

Long-time residents who sit on zoning commissions also face conflicts of interest. Because they usually have relatives who own land in the community, commissioners who are 'natives' frequently have to pass judgment on applications submitted by relatives. An incident in Cornwall suggests how intractable this problem can be. When the zoning commission considered a subdivision proposal submitted by a former first selectman, an exurbanite questioned the propriety of the commission's procedures because one of the commissioners was a relative of the developer. When the commission's chairman heard the complaint, he considered replacing the commissioner with an alternate until he learned that the alternate was also a relative of the developer.[33]

Recognition of the potential for conflicts of interest raises doubts about the possibility of administering zoning laws in a just fashion, and these doubts reduce rural residents' support for land-use laws. Oftentimes the administration of a new law is most effective when it does little more than reinforce preexisting relational controls over land use. Roxbury in the 1930s provides an example of this pattern of control. In 1932 the first selectman was a Hurlbut, a family with a large farm and 150 years of residence in Roxbury. The first selectman heard about zoning through his uncle, a public official in a suburb of Hartford. The idea appealed to him, so he used his considerable influence to get the Roxbury town council to pass an imprecisely worded ordinance which provided the first selectman with powers over land use in the community. Hurlbut proceeded to enforce this statute through visits to each building site in the town. Because Roxbury's population was only about 600 persons, it was a simple matter to visit each site and chat with the builder, whom Hurlbut invariably knew on a first name basis. During these visits the first selectmen would occasionally suggest a change in the blueprints which would reduce the interferences which the new building would cause neighboring landowners. Although Hurlbut made his suggestions in a friendly, informal way, they had the force of law. Both the first selectman's formal and informal position in the community contributed to his persuasiveness. The formal controls in Roxbury owed much of their effectiveness to preexisting relational controls.

Rule-based controls also prove effective when a change in land markets, coincident with a community's incorporation into a metropolitan area, brings outside developers into a community. Without the leverage or fund of good will enjoyed by local developers, outside developers usually face an unsympathetic commission. A long-time resident of Warren characterized Joseph Kavanewsky, an outside developer who specialized in large subdivisions, in these terms. "I don't think we should feel sorry for Mr. Kavanewsky. He's in business. It's like feeling sorry for A. T. & T."[34]

Outside developers come to the commission without political support and with a project which may arouse controversy because it departs from the existing pattern of land use. Under these circumstances the commissioners often deny permission to build. During the 1970s one town voted down a proposal to build a large subdivision of single-family homes along a lakeshore, and another town denied permission to build a low-income housing project. A third town rejected a proposal to turn a mansion into a religious retreat and denied permission to build a 240-unit townhouse development. In each instance a newcomer proposed a novel land use, and the new land use aroused the neighbors' apprehensions. Given the size of the projects and the developers' out-of-town origins, the neighbors knew that social pressure would not result in effective controls over land use. Under these circumstances rural residents begin to appreciate the value of rule-based controls over land use.

Land-use abuses and relational controls in rural communities

Despite the absence or near absence of controls over politically powerful landowners, rural communities do not invariably become the site of large-scale land abuses. Slow growth and the small size of markets limits the scale of land-use conversion. Developers build only one or two houses a year because the local housing market can not absorb more new housing. In most cases the small size of real estate developments and the presence of buffer zones prevents new developments from disrupting the use of nearby tracts of land. For example, a high percentage of the septic systems in northwestern Connecticut are defective, but complaints about defective septic systems rarely occur because seepage from the tanks usually occurs too far from the homes to bother anyone. A problem which might generate complaints in a suburb does not do so in a more spacious rural setting. Under these circumstances land-use conversion does not generate demands for legal controls over land use.

Relational controls over land use both lessen the need for formal controls and subvert the process of formal control when it first begins. Social pressures prevent local developers from abusing the land in the absence of legal controls. The prospect of face to face encounters between the builder and the homeowner gives the farmer-developer an incentive to build a house free of serious defects. Social pressures also prevent zoning commissioners from pursuing the public interest once legal controls have been enacted. A history of face to face encounters with applicants makes it difficult for a commissioner to judge their applications impartially. In this situation the old system of informal controls lives on in a new, formal guise. The social pressures which give influential landowners special advantages in determining their own and their neighbors' land uses under informal controls continue to give them advantages under formal controls. Without the social connections of local landowners, outside developers can resist efforts at informal control, but they cannot circumvent formal controls. For them the passage of a land-use law signals a real increase in restrictions on the use of land.

Relational controls not only work to reduce the number and magnitude of land-use abuses, they also reduce the number of land-use abuses which become public knowledge. When abuses occur and the injured parties are neighboring landowners with little influence in the community, they may be reluctant to complain. If the perpetrator is an influential landowner, complaints are especially unlikely. Land uses which would cause controversy in a suburban community produce "false unanimity" in rural locales.[35] In sum, rural communities have neither plans nor planners, but the shape of the land market, coupled with informal social controls, either limits abuses or suppresses knowledge of abuses when they occur. The distribution of power among local landowners determines which of these two effects will predominate in a place. Where the distribution of power among landowners is relatively equal and landowners have leverage over one another, clusters of cooperating landowners will develop informal controls over land use. Where the distribution of power among landowners is unequal, the powerful landowner will exert informal controls over his less powerful neighbors, but the neighbors will not exert the same control over his land uses. If the influential person's land uses have negative spillover effects, false unanimity may characterize attitudes about local land uses.

When communities are incorporated into a metropolitan area, new types of developers appear, the number and scale of real estate developments increases, and along with these changes comes a dramatic increase in publicly acknowledged land-use abuses. To curb the abuses and limit the number of conflicts, communities develop new controls over land use.

5 A rural–urban fringe community

Introduction

An extensive alluvial plain made New Milford a center for agricultural activities in western Connecticut in the nineteenth and twentieth centuries. In 1929 the town counted 55 farms within its borders; in 1974, after extensive suburban development, it still had 14 farms, but most of them figured in the plans of one or another developer. Rural to urban land-use conversion during the 1960s and early 1970s had already given the community a suburban appearance. Subdivisions of single-family homes dotted the landscape, a commercial strip lined a heavily traveled north–south highway, and a large landfill, known locally as 'Mt Trashmore', covered what had been a 150-acre farm.

Rapid land-use conversion, opportunism, and support for rule-based controls

In the fast changing but indeterminate environment of the rural–urban fringe, potentially incompatible land uses grow up together. Poor farmers' residences alternate with wealthy exurbanites' homes along the less-traveled roads while stores mix with houses along heavily traveled highways. In the Fox Hill area depicted in figure 7 one-time tenant farmers live in a cluster of trailers down one road while, 300 yards away, a wealthy stockbroker lives in a house on a hill. The variety of land uses generates uncertainty about future real estate development in an area. One developer plans to build modestly priced starter homes on a hillside while another developer talks about creating a trailer park, and a third developer considers building colonial homes on large lots, all on tracts of land within one-quarter mile of each other.

The rapid rate of real estate development sharpens peoples' concerns about the direction of development. Not only are the proposed real estate developments quite different in type, they are often built, one after the other,

72

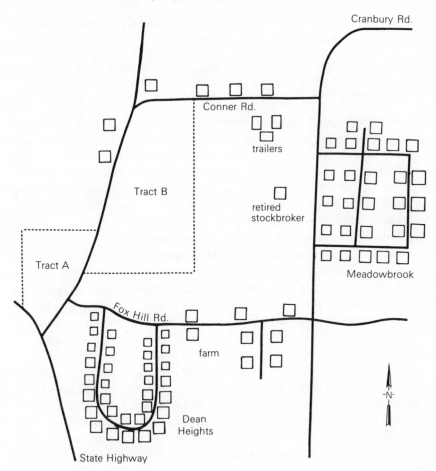

Figure 7 *The Fox Hill neighborhood*

in rapid succession. Development in these places may appear to be never-ending; one development, a subdivision of homes, creates the conditions for another development, a small shopping center, which in turn creates the conditions for a third development. In this atmosphere homeowners begin to think of urbanization almost organically, as a creature which moves across the landscape, ignoring town lines, converting land to intense uses, and spreading congestion, crime, and pollution wherever it goes. This view underlies the warnings issued in the middle of zoning controversies that, if policies do not change, "New Milford will become another White Plains" or "Newtown will become another Paramus."[1] Sometimes the predictions are more specific. For example, a Southbury homeowner argued that, if the town constructed a sewer through his neighborhood it

would be hard pressed...to stop motels, apartments, and assorted businesses from popping up all over the residential area along the sewer line. And, once the sewer line comes in, other sections of the town will get tied in too.[2]

This conception of suburban development assigns a crucial role to the expansion of infrastructure like roads or sewers. In controversies over highway construction in the mid 1970s, opponents of the new road referred to the "inexorable development pressure" created by the approach of the highway.[3] By shortening the travel time between centers of employment and the rural–urban fringe, new highways would make it possible for city workers to reside in hitherto inaccessible areas. The increased access would in turn raise land prices and stimulate building in the area. These arguments had a historical basis. The construction of I-84 in the early 1960s, I-684 in the late 1960s, and portions of Route 7 in the 1970s stimulated rapid changes in land values and encouraged speculation in land. Speculation changed the characteristics of the landowners. Farmers and exurbanites, who for sentimental reasons often would not sell, gave way to speculators, who would sell, which in turn increased the probability of rapid land-use conversion. In the late 1960s "half of New Milford was for sale."

The subsequent wave of real estate development made it easy for homeowners to imagine intense commercial, industrial, or residential land uses which, over a period of years, would invade their neighborhood, encroach on their homes, and, by impairing the residential atmosphere, cause a decline in property values. This view informed homeowner responses to proposals for development. For example, in 1974 a developer wanted to enlarge the parking lot behind his New Milford offices by cutting down a small patch of woods. Because the developer's proposal would have eliminated a strip of wooded land between his offices and nearby single-family homes, several homeowners opposed the proposal. Although one homeowner lived more than a quarter mile from the land in question, he objected to the parking lot extension on the grounds that "the developer had to be stopped now." In his words, "if you give developers an inch, they take a mile. Once they get started, there is no stopping them."[4] The homeowner anticipated that one rezoning would lead to a whole series of similar rezonings which eventually would convert his residential neighborhood into a commercial district. In his mind and the minds of other homeowners large changes in the character of a neighborhood often have small beginnings.

The fiscal crises in local government which accompanied the sweeping changes in land use added to the instability in land-use patterns. To resolve fiscal crises, politicians tried to convince tax-paying enterprises to locate in their communities. This policy brought additional tax revenues into the coffers of local government, but it also encouraged the expansion of commercial and industrial land uses into areas with homes. This policy and its effects caught homeowners in a contradiction epitomized by the activities of a young New Milford couple. While the wife lobbied for commercial and industrial expansion in an effort to reduce property taxes, the husband attended public hearings to voice his concern about the effects of commercial encroachment on their neighborhood.

Under these conditions an urban community with highly varied land uses began to emerge. One area became a high status neighborhood, another area became a slum, and a third area became a commercial or industrial strip. The wide range of outcomes increased the risks for property owners. They could commit large sums of money to a land use which, in the aftermath of nearby land-use conversions, could leave them with a deteriorating house in a mixed-use area of a vacant store in an overbuilt commercial strip. At the same time changes in the quality of land available for development added to the risks which developers faced. Builders quickly acquired and developed the 'easy' land in fringe communities, leaving only parcels which had problems with slope, ledge, or wetlands. Under these circumstances a builder's ability to turn a profit often hinged on his ability to develop the marginal lands in his subdivision.

The changes in land markets produce changes in developers. The increased value of land and the increased range of financial outcomes raises the stakes in the real estate game and encourages people to specialize in some aspect of real estate development. Full-time developers replace part-time farmers who also build houses as the prototypical developer in the community. Full-time developers are more mobile than part-time developers in at least two respects. First, full-time developers build in a larger geographical area. As the data on apartment construction presented in chapter 3 suggests, developers in fringe areas will shift their operations to other communities if the land markets or land-use regulations change in ways that disadvantage them. Secondly, as land begins to turn over at a higher rate, a developer's landholdings and the associated sets of neighboring landowners change more rapidly. In either sense the increase in the developers' mobility changes the land-use conversion situation from one which resembles an iterated social dilemma to one which resembles a single-play social dilemma. As Coleman and Axelrod have pointed out, this type of change should reduce the incidence of cooperative behavior. Applied to land-use conversion situations, this line of reasoning suggests that cost cutting practices which produce defects in construction and negative spillover effects on adjacent landowners would be more common among developers in fast-paced fringe land markets than they would be among developers in rural land markets.

Evidence which documents the developers' absence of concern about spillover effects or the quality of new construction is difficult to obtain, but evidence for one subset of accompanying behaviors does exist. When the noncooperative behavior involved deception, people took notice, and on occasion these practices became the object of public controversies. Interviews and newspaper articles yielded information about opportunistic behaviors by a wide variety of actors in rural–urban fringe real estate markets. Examples of these behaviors are outlined below.

The selection of a route for a limited access highway in the late 1960s prompted so much chicanery that the editors at the New Milford *Times* had to comment upon it.

Now let's take the shopping plaza. It is a beautiful piece of engineering in whatever sense of the word you choose. It has had problems from the beginning with the septic system, water pipes dumping water into the rear parking area, with stagnant water breeding contempt, if not mosquitos, at the rear of the property. It is truly a beauty, and we dare say that the owners are not dissolved in tears at the news that Rte. 7 will crush it to oblivion.

Then lets take the 'open spaces' once threatened by a proposed alternative route for the 'corridor'. Though open land, as opposed to mowing down 40 houses, has seemed most logical to us throughout, apparently it cannot be that simple. Weantinoge and Mr. Pratt have plans for that land, and according to Lambit Vehur, assistant chief of planning, "from higher ups we were told that we should avoid open spaces if we could because of the general local pressure on this matter." Must we come right out and say that we smell politics all the way, or perhaps we should just let our readers draw their own conclusions.[5]

The conversion of the Meadowbrook farm into a subdivision of single-family homes (see figure 7) provides another example of opportunistic behavior. In the late 1960s an elderly widow without heirs owned the farm. Her family had operated the farm since the early nineteenth century, and she wanted the land to remain in agriculture after her death. At the time she rented some acreage to a prominent local farmer who pastured his cattle and grew hay on the land. The widow had willed the farm to the Methodist Church, but, after the farmer promised to give the land to his youngest son to work, the widow changed her will so that, upon her death, the farmer could purchase the farm for a low price. When the widow died, the farmer exercised his option to purchase the land and reneged on his promise to the widow. Within six months of purchasing the land, he had sold it to a developer and, with the proceeds from the sale, purchased a much larger farm in southwestern Virginia.[6]

Builders engage in a variety of opportunistic practices. In 1979 the SKG corporation, an out of town developer, presented the zoning commission with maps which indicated that portions of a subdivision were in one zone when they were in another zone. This oversight enabled SKG to put more units on the land than the regulations permitted. The following year the same developer failed to show wetlands on the maps of another subdivision and flushed suspect wells before conducting sanitary tests on them. In another instance SKG concealed the ownership of adjacent properties and at different times presented the commission with separate plans for developing small, but contiguous parcels of land. Taken in by this strategy, the commission allowed the construction of long driveways into the inner lots of each parcel. In this manner the developer avoided the expense of constructing a subdivision road in the area.[7]

Paul Vierra encountered opportunism in purchasing a home. The real estate agent, who sold Mr. Vierra the house, made the following statements before the sale.

1 Dartmouth Road (the road Mr. Vierra's house was on) would be finished that year and...it would be accepted into the town highway system right away.
2 No factory would be built nearby because the town is zoned.
3 Travel time to White Plains (where Mr. Vierra works) would be very short. "I can get to Manhattan in 45 minutes," said the agent.
4 The new Route 7 will pass several hundred yards in back of the development...then it will take you even less time to get to White Plains.[8]

In his eagerness to make the sale, the realtor misled Mr. Vierra. The subdivision road was not accepted into the town highway system in the next year, the community had no zoning law, the driving time to New York City was at least twice the realtor's estimate, and, while the eventual route of Route 7 had not been decided upon, at least one proposed route went right through Mr. Vierra's lot. Mr. Vierra concluded, charitably, that

the agent's major fault was his overly definite statement about everything. If he had only said "I think," it wouldn't have been such a misrepresentation of fact.[9]

Opportunism also surfaces in the plans which homeowners make to sell their homes. For example, after hearing in mid-winter about plans for a nearby commercial development, a young couple decided to sell their house.

Several days later they reconsidered and decided to hold the house off the market until the late spring. In the winter the traffic on Route 7 is clearly audible and visible through the bare trees behind the house. These conditions change in April and May with the growth of a luxuriant green wall of leaves on the trees. The leaves obstruct the view and muffle the sounds coming from the road, so prospective homeowners do not realize how close the house is to Route Seven. Accordingly, the couple expected summer buyers to offer them more money than winter buyers, and on this basis they postponed the sale of their home until the summer.[10]

The unpleasant surprises which await parties to real estate transactions in the fringe communities sometimes stem, not from deceitful behavior, but from ignorance about local trends in land use. Realtors, who usually provide outside buyers with this information, are often misinformed. Patterns of recruitment into the real estate profession explain the realtors' ignorance. To become a realtor in the late 1970s in Connecticut, an individual had to take a six-week course in real estate, purchase $14.95 in books, and pay the state $100 for a license. This small investment gave individuals the opportunity to share in the large profits generated by the high turnover of land in fringe communities. The potential for high profits, coupled with the low entry costs and the part-time nature of the work, made real estate an attractive occupation in fringe communities. As a result individuals often entered the profession without knowing much about land use, and inevitably they made mistakes in arranging transactions in land. For example, in the Meadow-brook subdivision (see figure 7) a realtor sold a lot with a subterranean stream to a couple who wanted to build a home. Either the realtor did not know of the stream's existence or she did not realize that its presence would prevent building on the lot. Because the couple could not build on the land, they sued the realtor for damages.[11]

A lack of knowledge about local landowners, in addition to a lack of technical expertise, contributes to the realtors' failure to provide accurate information. The realtors' brief residence in the community accounts for their lack of knowledge. Unlike realtors in slow-growing communities, realtors in fast-growing fringe communities are often newcomers to the community. The recent purchase of a house stimulates the newcomer's interest in real estate, and the rapid turnover of land generates jobs for the newcomers on the staffs of established realtors. Because the new realtors do not have an extensive set of contacts in the community, they usually do not know much about the local farmers' personal situations. Without this information, realtors cannot predict when a farmer will sell to developers and cannot tell prospective purchasers whether or not the land behind a house will be developed in the next few years. To make a sale, a realtor may still try to impress potential purchasers with the stability of land uses in a neighborhood. If the buyers believe the realtor, subsequent events may surprise them. The experience of a new homeowner in the Meadowbrook subdivision is typical. In the three-year period after the realtor promised the homeowner that the land behind the house would never be developed, the land changed hands several times and with each sale came a new set of rumors about plans for developing the property.[12]

In a real estate market in which rapid, thoroughgoing changes in land use appear imminent, information about neighboring land users is difficult to obtain, and stories about opportunistic landowners are legion, homeowners become apprehensive about the direction of development in their neighborhood. They respond to the perceived threats both individually and collectively. Individually, they try to trade up. In so doing, they vie with other individuals for an advantageous position in the emerging residential mosaic. Collectively, they argue for a simple exclusionary law which, by prohibiting the construction of everything but expensive single-family homes, should over time establish the upper-class character of their neighborhood.

While the creation of exclusionary rules represents an unmistakable shift in the form of land-use control, two related phenomena limit the impact of the change. First, the substance of the laws varies across neighborhoods with some neighborhoods receiving little regulation. Secondly, important aspects of the land-use conversion process, such as the quality of new construction, fall outside the regulatory reach of the laws and must be controlled, if at all, through face-to-face interactions.

Neighborhood activists, implementation, and uneven development

The adoption of a land-use law does not imply its implementation; a law's implementation, like its adoption, involves a political struggle whose outcome depends largely on the level of homeowner support for the law. The history of real estate development in the Fox Hill neighborhood illustrates how homeowners can shape the substance of the law and how the law, once it is in place, can change the character of a neighborhood. Homeowners on Fox Hill have strong reservations about developments which promise to depress the value of their homes. Out of a series of developments proposed for Fox Hill during the 1960s and 1970s, only two, a mobile home park and an apartment complex, might have caused declines in the property values of nearby single-family homes. Rumors about the proposed mobile home park surfaced shortly after the adoption of zoning, during deliberations about regulations for the neighborhood. After hearing the rumors, homeowners from the Dean Heights subdivision (see figure 7) attended a public hearing and registered their objections to the mobile homes. They argued for regulations which, by prohibiting everything but single-family homes in the Fox Hill area, would make it impossible for the developer to build the proposed project. The zoning commissioners adopted these regulations. When the proposal came up for discussion several months later, the residents argued and the commissioners agreed that a mobile home park would be inconsistent with the land-use plan for the area.

Fox Hill residents first became aware of the apartment proposal through an announcement in the obscure, hard-to-read legal notices section of the local newspaper. In an apprehensive tone of voice one New Milford resident recalled how,

If it had not been for Peter reading the fine print in the *Times*, we never would have found out about the developer until it was too late.[13]

After learning of the proposed development, the nearby homeowners formed a residential association, hired a lawyer to represent them, and turned out in large numbers for the hearing. The first speaker at the hearing, the homeowners' lawyer, set the tone for subsequent speakers by making an impassioned argument that the commission should deny the application in order to preserve the peace and quiet of his clients' lives. The developer's lawyer followed with an equally emotional plea on behalf of the young people who might live in the apartments. After the lawyers had spoken, the commissioners opened the meeting up to the public, and a long procession of homeowners, most of them women, proceeded to speak with feeling about how the traffic around the apartments would disrupt domestic life in the adjacent single-family homes. Particularly impassioned remarks drew rounds of applause from other homeowners. At one point the developer got up, said a few words on behalf of his project, and sat down again. After about one and one-half hours of testimony the meeting broke up. The homeowners left quickly, stopping only for brief chats in the halls or outside the building with neighbors they knew. The developer and his associates lingered in the meeting room, ostensibly to ask the commissioners about changes in the technical details of the plan. The details which were not resolved in these conversations would be discussed the following day over the telephone or in a private meeting with the town planner.

Developers clearly prefer private meetings. Behind closed doors developers and commissioners speak more freely, and propositions, legal and illegal, are more forthcoming. In addition the numerous small conversations about changes in the technical details of a plan provide the developer with opportunities to impress the commissioners with the value of the overall plan. Homeowners' coalitions prefer public hearings. In public forums the homeowners can impress the commission with their large numbers. Extensive accounts of the hearings in the local press add to the political pressure on the commissioners. Under these circumstances the commissioners usually bow to political pressure, as they did in the Fox Hill case, and limit development in an area.

Fox Hill residents not only wanted their neighborhood to be a residential zone, they wanted it to be a residential zone for the rich. More specifically, most Fox Hill residents lived in homes on half-acre lots, but they wanted their future neighbors to live in larger homes on one- and two-acre lots. To this end Fox Hill residents argued for large minimum lot and floor areas in public hearings. The commissioners acceded to the residents' wishes in drawing up the regulations. To meet the new requirements, Fox Hill developers increased the size of the homes in new subdivisions and altered the pattern of construction in the old subdivisions. The quality of the homes in the new subdivisions convinced developers that they could build large, expensive homes next to small, starter homes in the old subdivisions and still sell the new homes. Accordingly, developers began constructing more expensive homes on the remaining undeveloped lots in the old subdivisions. In Dean Heights the developer began by building bungalows and finished by building more spacious ranches. At Meadowbrook the developers began the subdivision building six-room starter homes and finished the subdivision building eight-room custom built homes. In this incremental fashion a neighborhood emerged with a higher social status than one would have expected given the initial heterogeneous mix of land uses in the area. When the early settlers on Fox Hill sold their homes, they capitalized on the increased social status by selling for higher prices than they could have otherwise.

The pursuit of residential exclusivity had its limits. For many Fox Hill residents these limits were reached in 1977 when a developer proposed to build 'Pleasant View', a large subdivision of expensive single-family homes on Tract B in figure 6. When a prominent homeowner, Mr. C. V. Black, conducted a door-to-door canvas of his neighbors in an attempt to organize opposition to the proposed development, a number of his neighbors demurred. As one resident put it, "I worked my way up from New York, and others are entitled to do the same thing."[14] The construction of new housing did not bother these residents as long as the new homes promised to elevate and not depress the value of their homes. Because the large homes proposed for the 'Pleasant View' development seemed likely to add to the value of nearby homes, many Fox Hill residents were reluctant to oppose the project.

Not every neighborhood in a fast-growing community follows the course of development of Fox Hill. While some areas rise in social status, others fall. Administrative practices in the absence of popular pressure for restrictive controls explain why development takes a different path in politically unorganized neighborhoods.

Simple procedures govern the administration of land-use laws in fringe communities. Builders bring completed plans for developing a particular tract of land to their first meeting with the planning and zoning commission. After going over the plans briefly, the commission gives them to a planning consultant for further scrutiny. The consultant, who typically spends two or three days a month in the community on a retainer paid by the commission, examines the plans for several weeks. If the developer has complied with the zoning regulations and the health district requirements, the consultant usually recommends that the commission approve the subdivision, and the commission does so. As one town planner put it,

If the plans are in order, there really is not much that can be done to stop the developer from subdividing the land and building the homes.[15]

Virtually no negotiations occur between the developer and the commissioner prior to the submission of the plans. These procedures reflect the projects to be regulated. The small scale of most projects limits their impact on public services, and the spacious layouts within each subdivision reduce the probability of water and sewage problems. In sum, most projects do not promise to generate serious social or environmental problems, so sustained contact between developers and planners seems superfluous.

When developments depart from the small, spacious scale, as they do with increasing frequency in fringe communities, the pattern of administration usually remains the same even though the projects' potential environmental impacts are much greater. The routine treatment accorded these projects may be explicable in terms of the commissioners' favorable attitudes toward development. Their occupational histories and business associations predispose them to look favorably on new developments. Former farmers, whose lands had been developed for single-family homes, held important political positions in New Milford during the 1960s and 1970s. In developer–homeowner controversies these politicians found the developer's point of view easy to understand. Their business activities also worked in the developer's favor. For instance, the first chairman of the planning and zoning commission was a prominent banker in the community. One evening, as he and a fellow commissioner walked across the green to the town hall, the chairman remarked that the developers whose application the commission was to consider that evening had come to him the previous week for a loan to finance the development and that he considered them to be 'responsible' developers whose application should be approved.[16] The pro-developer bias illustrated here appears common among land-use authorities in former farming communities.

The bias does not show up so much in what the commission chooses to do as in what it chooses not to do. Plans for development in which the developer has incentives to cut corners receive no more scrutiny than do other plans for development. After a few perfunctory interactions the developers receive permission to build. Plans for development which promise to interfere with neighboring landowners only get special attention when the neighbors protest, as they did in the Fox Hill neighborhood.[17]

Even if the commissioners had wanted to exercise close control over developers, the meager resources devoted to land-use planning in New Milford would have made restrictive regulation difficult, if not impossible, to carry out. The land-use authorities were all volunteers, most of whom held full-time jobs. Constraints on their time created by obligations to employers and families shaped the commissioners' approach to land-use control. They practiced 'negative' planning. They spent most of their time reviewing subdivision proposals, and little time "planning for the needs of the town."[18] Time constraints also affected the review of proposals. As the editorial writers for the local newspaper put it, the commission "does not have the time or expertise to check out every aspect of every application."[19] Under these circumstances the commissioners frequently do not visit the sites for proposed developments, do not monitor construction sites with periodic inspections, and fail to act quickly in response to complaints about a developer's work. In defense of this record the chairman of the commission pointed out that "we're all volunteers; we can't sit here and answer the phone all day."[20] The town's building and health code administrators are full-time employees, but the large volume of building in the town makes it difficult for them to carry out more than cursory inspections of new construction. Under these circumstances town officials must rely on the developer to carry out the plans approved by the commission. For example, the town allows developers to conduct the water quality tests on the wells in their subdivisions. The town sanitarian outlined the assumptions behind this procedure, "All I can do is take the analysis over his [the developer's] signature and trust that it's for the lot that it's said to be."[21]

Town officials rely on trust in other situations. In the late 1970s the first chairman of the planning and zoning commission decided to become a developer and resigned his position on the commission. Several months later he appeared before the commission as an applicant seeking approval for a low-income housing project. He received permission to go ahead with the project after agreeing informally to reserve the new housing for the elderly. Several years later when the ex-commissioner failed to keep his word, the local newspaper chastised the commissioners for making informal agreements with developers.[22]

Contacts between town officials and developers raise questions about the direction of the informal controls. Do commissioners control the developer or vice versa? After the building inspector took a Florida vacation on a developer's yacht and the zoning inspector had work done on his home by the same developer's subcontractor, several citizens argued in the local press that the town should have a code of ethics to govern contacts between town officials and developers. The Board of Selectmen rejected the idea; after the meeting one selectman explained his opposition. "It [the code of ethics] gives me a feeling that we mistrust our employees."[23] This reliance on trust represents a continued resort to relational controls in the regulation of real estate development, albeit in a more limited set of circumstances than in rural communities. In the fast paced rural–urban fringe land market the developer has more incentives to betray this trust, and land-use problems occur more frequently.

In sum the local officials' pro-developer bias, coupled with the meager resources devoted to land-use planning, minimize the effects of land-use laws in fringe areas. In this setting rule-based controls only have an exclusionary impact in those neighborhoods in which the residents stand ready to defend the rules. As the data on opposition to development reported in table 8 indicate, organized opposition to development is more the exception than the rule in New Milford land-use planning. Throughout the 1970s editorials in the New Milford *Times* complained about citizen apathy, and developers expressed genuine surprise when their plans for a subdivision encountered opposition from nearby homeowners.[24]

Builders, buyers, and the persistence of relational controls

The number of development-induced environmental problems varies, like opposition to development, from neighborhood to neighborhood in New Milford. The variation in the incidence of environmental problems is somewhat surprising because the enforcement of land-use regulations is lax throughout the town. As indicated above, the zoning enforcement officer and the building inspector limit their efforts at enforcement to cursory, on-site inspections of buildings under construction. Although developers must post a bond which they cannot collect until the town has approved the buildings for use, New Milford officials have never withheld the bond from a developer accused of shoddy construction.

The geographical variations in development-induced environmental problems originate in differences between builders in their ability to take advantage of lax enforcement. In general builders are quite conservative in the conduct of their business. They learn how to do one type of real estate development, small subdivisions of single-family homes, for instance, and they continue to do that type of development as long as economic conditions permit (Kenney, 1972:168). By implication a pronounced change in the type of development, as occurs in rural–urban fringe communities, entails a change in the builders who work in the community. In some areas, usually the hilly, upper-income neighborhoods, the scale of real estate development remains unchanged. Builders, who established themselves in the community before the beginning of rapid real estate development, continue to build small numbers of homes, but they build for an increasingly affluent clientele. In areas with an abundance of flat, well-drained land, out of town developers begin to build. These developers, attracted by the large number of building sites in a single area, specialize in building large subdivisions of inexpensive single-family homes. The data on subdivision activities in 1979 reflect the differences between builders. Subdivisions proposed by local builders averaged five houses in size; subdivisions proposed by outside developers averaged 40 houses in size.[25] Differences between the two types of developers in their relations with prospective homeowners probably account for most of the local variation in environmental problems.

The builder–buyer relationship in upper-income neighborhoods

Because the scale of development in affluent neighborhoods does not change appreciably as a small town becomes a suburb, changes in the type of developer do not occur in these areas. The same developers continue to build small numbers of single-family homes, but the homes tend to be more expensive than the first homes which they constructed in the area. The change in the price of housing stems in part from a change in the type of buyer looking for housing. Increasing numbers of these prospective purchasers want to trade up to a custom-built home.

Trading up takes several forms depending on the wealth of the purchasers.

For some households it means moving from a small house, indistinguishable from the neighboring houses except in color, to a larger home set at an angle on a larger lot and surrounded by homes of a different style. Other households want to move out of a development altogether. These households regard their new home as "the last house which we will build." Both types of homeowners who trade up take an active interest in the construction of their new homes. Many of them make daily trips to the construction site to check on the builder's progress. With this type of surveillance, developers are reluctant to try significant short cuts in the construction of the houses. What is more, if a potentially costly problem arises during the construction of the house, the builder and buyer can confer and decide on a course of action. Because the builder wants to get paid, the buyer has the influence necessary for the effective exercise of relational controls over land use. As a result custom built homes have relatively few defects.

Spacious layouts and small numbers of homes reduce the number of environmental problems in high status subdivisions. Take roads for example. Large-scale developers are likely to cut corners in road construction because the roads belong to no one and are completed after all of the houses in the development have been sold. The problems with these roads often become evident after only a few months of use. The residents of small-scale developments encounter road problems less frequently. Small-scale developers usually build on undeveloped lots along town roads, so no road has to be built. If a road is built, it is often deeded over to a residential association which, within limits set by local fire districts, keeps the roads up to standards set by the homeowners. Sewage provides another example of the low potential for problems in spacious subdivisions. The rugged topography in these subdivisions makes it difficult to find a suitable place to sink a septic system on a lot, but the lots in these subdivisions are so large that an acceptable site for a septic system can almost always be found. Under these circumstances homeowners face few septic problems.

The builder–buyer relationship in middle-income neighborhoods

Developers in middle-income neighborhoods build starter homes and sell them in markets in which buyers are very price conscious. Starter home developers make profits if they keep their prices low, sell large numbers of homes, and skimp in the construction of the less obvious parts of the home. The skimping frequently includes 'shortcuts' such as spacing the nails at wide intervals on the hidden seams, failing to put gravel on the driveway before paving it, and reducing the size of the gravel bed beneath the septic tank.

The young couples who purchase these homes have never owned homes before and know little about the mechanics of construction, sewage disposal, and water supply. On occasion this lack of knowledge has caused new homeowners some embarrassment. In one instance several new homeowners hooked up their dishwashers and washing machines to their septic systems. The detergent used in these machines was apparently strong enough to kill the bacteria which break down the feces in the septic tank. After a period of especially frequent washing in one house, the unprocessed sewage backed up enough to contaminate the washing machines and basement.[26] The first-home purchasers' ignorance about house and household technology makes it especially unlikely that they will detect defects in the construction of a house before they purchase it. Reinforcing their lack of knowledge is a lack of interest. Because first-time buyers are usually not as wealthy as other buyers, they show more interest in the financial aspects of a purchase and less interest in the quality of the construction than do other buyers.

Without relational controls or strictly enforced rule-based controls the builder–buyer relationship between outside developers and first-home purchasers generates a fantastic array of environmental problems. The history of the Dean Heights subdivision illustrates the range of environmental problems which can arise in these subdivisions. From its outset Dean Heights was plagued with problems. The subdivision sits on the side of a hill which slopes sharply down to a state highway. In order to set the foundations of the houses and install septic systems in this terrain, the developer had to dig out a small terrace on each lot. The terracing increased the pitch of the land from the subdivision road down to the houses and from the back of the houses down to the state highway. In 1967 heavy rains on steep slopes of freshly moved earth caused a mud slide which blocked the state highway for several days. Each winter after snow or ice storms residents park their cars in the street because their driveways are too steep to negotiate under the icy conditions. When the police order the parked cars off the streets to facilitate snow plowing, the Dean Heights residents have nowhere to put their cars, and they get ticketed.

This last problem arose only after a persistent campaign by one homeowner had resulted in the acceptance of their road into the publically maintained system of roads. When the road was built in the mid 1960s, the town had a backlog of unaccepted roads awaiting inspection, so town officials refused to accept the Dean Heights road. With a promise that they would consider the road at a later date, they put it on a waiting list. Until that date the developer agreed to maintain the road with funds which he would collect from the homeowners. The developer never attempted to collect, the homeowners did not pay, and the road deteriorated. Several years later when the road came up for consideration by the town, the planning and zoning commission refused to accept it because it did not meet minimal standards in road building. After several more years of deteriorating conditions, a housewife in the subdivision went to the selectman to complain about the condition of the road. "In the very beginning he [the first selectman] would just sit there and chew his gum." Later on "he would talk to you like you didn't pay taxes."[27] The housewife persisted; she began going to every planning and zoning meeting to protest the condition of the road. After nine months of attending meetings, she apparently disturbed town officials enough to get them to negotiate an agreement with the developer in which he agreed to upgrade the road to the town's standards.

Dean Heights also has a sewage problem. The developer minimized expenses on the septic system by limiting the size of the septic fields beneath the tanks. Because the houses and septic fields sit on a ridge with compacted soils, the soils do not absorb the sewage and periodic back ups occur. Because the homes, like most starter homes, are built on small lots, buffer zones between the homes and the septic tanks do not exist, and on hot summer nights the residents have reason to complain about the smell of effluent.

The subdivision has also suffered from water problems. Rather than install a well for each house, the developer at Dean Heights established a community well. By not having to provide space on each lot for a well, the developer could reduce the size of each lot to the point where he could fit several more building lots onto the tract of land. During the construction of the subdivision the local board of health regulated the construction of wells in dilatory fashion. The regulations were vague, and there was no inspection of newly constructed wells; in effect, the developer did not have to conform to any standards. After he completed the well, the developer sold it to a business associate who lived approximately 20 miles from the development. For the next ten years the residents of the subdivision went without water for up to 12 hours at a time when the well broke down and the owner, living a good distance away, did not repair it. Eventually the residents formed an association in order to correct the water problem, and after threatening the owner with a lawsuit, they were able to acquire the well and make the necessary repairs on it.[28]

When problems occur, local government officials play an important role in their resolution. The controversy over the acceptance of the roads in the Camelot subdivision illustrates the pivotal role which local officials can play in dealing with these problems. The developers bought the land for Camelot from important political figures in New Milford. As usual the town did not immediately accept the subdivision's roads into the town system, so the developers remained responsible for the maintenance of the roads. When the developers were slow to plow out the subdivision after a snowstorm in 1969, Camelot residents began agitating to have the roads taken over by the town. In response to these political pressures the first selectman, the son of a farmer–developer, went up to the development, 'eyeballed' the roads, and decided that they met the minimum standards necessary for acceptance as town roads. The selectman then convinced the planning commission to accept the roads even though the commission had initially ruled against acceptance. This resolution then went to the town meeting for final approval. At the meeting two town residents, both of them engineers employed by the state highway department, objected to the acceptance of the roads, claiming on the basis of a cursory inspection that the roads did not meet the town's minimal standards. After this presentation the town meeting voted not to accept the roads. The dispute over the roads dragged on for several months, with the two engineers receiving threatening phone calls, until the bankers backing the Camelot developers became concerned over the prospect of deteriorating roads hindering the sale of homes in the subdivision. With this concern in mind, the bankers persuaded the developers to improve the roads to the point where the town would accept them.[29] The subsequent improvements ended the controversy.

The history of this incident demonstrates the power of elected officials in decisions about the environmental problems which result from uncontrolled development. Presumably the developers' political influence in the community predisposed the first selectman to accept the roads, and, once he had made up his mind to accept the roads, he was able to push his decision through the planning commission. Only the unusual intervention of two 'expert' citizens prevented the town from accepting cheaply built, defective roads. In this and other instances the inability of middle-income homeowners to exercise effective relational controls over developers, coupled with the continued predominance of the farmer-developer faction in local government, gives large scale developers the license to build inexpensive, but poorly constructed homes in rural–urban fringe communities.[30]

Land-use conversion, abuse, and control in a fringe community

The wave of land-use conversions which marks the incorporation of a rural community into a metropolitan area generates demands for land-use controls. Rising rates of turnover in land and mobility among residents increase the proportion of neighboring landowners who have only short-term interests in one another. According to arguments developed in chapter 2, this shift in relations between landowners should increase the incidence of noncooperative behaviors between landowners. Reliable and valid measures of these behaviors are difficult to obtain, but a variety of incidents recounted in interviews and newspapers strongly suggest that a rash of noncooperative, sometimes opportunistic, behaviors did occur in New Milford as the community was incorporated into the New York metropolitan area in the 1970s. In response to revelations about these behaviors, growing numbers of citizens decided that "there ought to be a law," and in a referendum they voted for legal controls over land use.

Several conditions limit the impact of the laws. Because the commissioners only enact simple, exclusionary rules when the residents of a neighborhood request them, the restrictive rules apply to some but not all neighborhoods. While the rules channel intense land uses away from some neighborhoods, they do not insure the quality of new construction in any of the neighborhoods. Under these circumstances informal social controls exercised by individual homeowners become important in determining the incidence of land-use abuses, and once again the wealthier individuals appear to exercise more effective control over land use. Because wealthy landowners who build custom homes usually choose scenic house sites in neighborhoods with restrictive land-use regulations, the differential exercise of homeowner control produces spatial variations in the incidence of environmental problems. Problems occur frequently in middle-class neighborhoods and rarely in upper-class neighborhoods.

As rural–urban fringe communities become more built up, differences between neighborhoods in the extent of citizen participation begin to decline. As newly settled, middle-income neighborhoods age, homeowners get to know one another, and their friendships become the basis for mobilizing opposition to proposed developments. New neighborhood associations provide the organizational basis for further opposition, and the knowledge of the planning process gained in the first protest provides a stimulus for further involvement. As one New Milford homeowner put it,

This is really the first time I've gotten into anything like this, but now that I've seen what can happen, I can see myself getting a lot more interested and involved in future issues.[31]

Neighborhoods with long histories of citizen activism also show signs of change. Residents in these neighborhoods begin to argue that simple, exclusionary rules often prevent effective land-use planning. Mrs. Alison Strong, the leader of homeowner opposition to the proposed Pleasant View subdivision on Fox Hill, expressed this view.

Physically, the proposed Pleasant View development ... may be just as outdated now as Dean Heights was 10 years ago. I can't blame the developer, though, for his conceptual approach to this project. The first time I ever encountered one of his representatives at the site, the gentleman told me that the original idea had been to submit a cluster-housing plan, and the town wouldn't hear of it. The zoning rules have us all boxed in to 18th century solutions for 20th century problems ... Instead of starting with a development plan and trying to mold the peculiar conditions of the site to fit it, start with the conditions and let them mold the development plan. Allow time, if necessary, for architects knowledgeable in community development to review the findings and make suggestions for a plan that will give the developer and the community something to be proud of. Something exceptionally interesting and profitable might emerge by finding the best use for this excellent piece of hillside land.[32]

In affluent urban communities planners take Mrs. Strong's recommendations to heart.

6 Urban communities

Introduction: a history of development

The two communities under study, Westport and Norwalk, are situated next to one another on the coast in southwestern Connecticut. They both began to experience suburban development in the 1930s. Over the next 30 years as developers in both communities converted large tracts of land to more intense uses, the land-use patterns in the two communities diverged. Westport evolved into an affluent suburb and Norwalk became a satellite city. In the 1970s, with little undeveloped land left, the two communities entered a period of slow growth. Both communities lost population between 1970 and 1980 as declines in household size more than offset modest increases in housing units.[1]

In the late 1920s Westport developers began erecting beach houses next to the large waterfront homes of summer residents. To preserve their seclusion, the summer residents campaigned for and succeeded in obtaining a zoning law to control shoreline development. A decade later, with the construction of the Merritt Parkway out from New York City, commuters began to settle in Westport and developers began to build single-family homes to accommodate the newcomers. Throughout the 1940s and 1950s plans to build single-family homes stimulated concern about land use. Rumors about proposals for large subdivisions sparked efforts by nearby homeowners to protect the 'country' atmosphere by increasing the land area required for new houses in their neighborhood. Rumors of up-zonings in turn stimulated bursts of activity by developers who wanted to submit their plans under the old, more permissive regulations. In several instances controversies developed over whether or not a builder had submitted his plan before the old regulations expired. In the early 1950s homeowners, in an attempt to gain more control over land-use conversion, began to lobby for the creation of a master plan and the use of planning consultants to guide the commission in implementing the plan. In a planning commission survey 38 percent of Westport's residents objected to these innovations. Predictably, the opposition concentrated among the locally employed, long-term residents of the town.[2]

The local newspaper described the configuration of conflicting interests in a front page editorial on a related dispute over Westport's schools.

The controversy over the schools' budget makes clear that there is a basic conflict of opinion... between two groups of town citizens. One group tends to want a top flight residential town, with strict zoning to keep out any and all industry and to prevent 'development' buildings, with superior schools and services and with all the other luxuries and services (like space and air and civic beauty) that fewer and fewer towns think that they can afford. These are not all high income people. They are simply men and women who are willing to pay a disproportionately high percentage of whatever income they have for better schools and a better environment for themselves and for their children. ... There is another group to whom a low tax rate is more important than some of these other things... The group is divided into a number of subgroups with dissimilar motives. There are those individuals whose children are beyond school age and who feel that they should be finished paying school bills. There are those who believe that everything beyond reading, writing, and 'rithmetic constitutes unnecessary frills in education. There are those who own real property as an investment, who thus have a greater stake in the tax rate than those who pay it only upon their living place. There are those whose short-term business success depends on a large population per se... These are not all low income people by any means. The big real estate owner may be the wealthiest man in town.

Group 1 may be a majority in the town, but group 2 is formidable because they control most of the paraphernalia of power... This is the most important issue which Westport will face in many a year. This is the basic question in Westport's growth. The growth is inevitable. The direction of growth is in question. Is Westport to be an ideal living place with the schools, space, and planned services that make life worthwhile? Or is Westport to be just another 'Topsy' town, trying to enjoy low taxes and quick development at the same time, and willingly sacrificing school standards and zoning regulations in the process.[3]

This controversy was one of a series whose outcomes over a 40 year period determined the direction of development in Westport. A number of the controversies ended with changes in the land-use laws. Regulations introduced in the 1930s made it difficult for industries to locate in Westport. An amendment in the 1950s prohibited the construction of multi-family housing. Other amendments increased the minimum lot areas for single-family homes, making the construction of inexpensive homes impossible. By the late 1950s the combined effect of these changes had earned Westport a reputation as one of the most exclusive communities in southwestern Connecticut. As this reputation emerged, self-selection among in-migrants increased. Businessmen interested in building expensive homes looked for land in Westport. High-priced boutiques and speciality shops sought out

Westport locations in order to be close to their clientele. Over a 15 year period, between 1950 and 1965, selective in-migration transformed Westport into one of the wealthiest communities in southwestern Connecticut.

This pattern of growth changed the residents' conception of their community. In 1954 editorial writers for the local newspaper could conclude that

So far we have been able to muddle through pretty well. No one can rightly criticize the general state of Westport, as towns go. Our zoning is reasonably adequate, although certainly not impossible of improvement. Our schools compare favorably, so far, with those of our neighbors.[4]

These writers convey an impression of a community which is slightly better but not essentially different from its neighbors. In 20 years' time, after extensive but selective real estate development, the chairman of the planning and zoning commission described the town in different terms.

We have painted our future in Westport as a nice, quiet, little old town; we think of ourselves, or some do, as a mini-Paris on the Saugatuck [here she was interrupted by laughter], with painters painting and writers writing and strollers, and not much change since the days of the onion farm...We are distinct from our neighbors and maybe this is the greatest service that this town can perform for the region.[5]

To preserve the special character of the place, citizens, merchants, and politicians exercised close control over land-use conversion. They made policy for a community which experienced declines in the rate of real estate development during the 1960s and 1970s. While the construction of office complexes increased during this period, the construction of single-family homes declined sharply. The average number of housing units constructed each year dropped 70 percent between 1960 and 1980.[6] The slowdown had its origins in the growing scarcity of land suitable for single-family homes. Builders who specialized in large subdivisions left Westport because they could no longer find tracts of land for 30 and 40 home subdivisions. Only small-scale residential developers continued to build in the town.

While Norwalk, like Westport, adopted its first zoning law in the late 1920s and experienced its first wave of suburban development in the 1930s, it did not experience, as Westport did, the same trends in land-use conversion throughout the community. In Norwalk the trends varied from neighborhood to neighborhood. In the centrally located districts working-class homeowners tried to ease their financial burden by converting single-family homes into two-family homes. In the outlying districts landowners proposed income-producing uses for residential properties less frequently, and, when they did, their proposals met with opposition from nearby homeowners. At a public hearing on a proposed art supply store in Silvermine, a residential area in northwestern Norwalk, a prominent homeowner explained why he opposed commercial land uses.

our interests rest in the protection of sections like Silvermine. Darien, Westport, and other surrounding places are talking Norwalk down as a place to reside. They are saying that Norwalk is a good industrial area but a poor residential area. In (our own) defense we must protect our residential areas.[7]

The neighbors' opinions often proved decisive in deciding a case for or against an applicant. In the early 1940s the Zoning Board of Appeals tended to approve noncontroversial conversions and deny controversial conversions.[8] Because conversions in the outlying residential districts encountered opposition while those in the center city did not, only the center city conversions received approval. Under the impact of these decisions land-use patterns began to diverge from one another. The centrally located neighborhoods began to develop into densely populated, low-income areas while the peripheral neighborhoods began to evolve into exclusive residential areas.

The differences grew more pronounced after World War II. The planning and zoning commission failed to exert any control over land-use changes in the centrally located industrial areas.

The heavy industrial zone is like no zone. Heavy industrial number one [zone] is a little more restrictive than nothing.[9]

As a result the industrial areas developed into "a hodge podge of office, commercial, retail, and residential uses."[10] Property owners in these districts continued to press for increased densities throughout the 1950s. Homeowners and small businessmen, with names such as Kazarian and Coachia, stood before commissioners with names such as Howard and Seymour and asked for permission to subdivide their homes, create dwellings in garages, or convert the first floor of a home into a restaurant. In numerous cases the commissioners found hardship and approved the applications.[11]

Nearby, in recently completed residential subdivisions homeowners began to discover structural defects in their homes and landscaping problems on their lots. In several cases homeowners complained to the authorities when the developers refused to do additional drainage work around the new homes.[12] Conflicts broke out over plans for development on lands bordering the new subdivisions. On several occasions homeowners accused developers of misleading them about plans for developing nearby tracts of land.[13] These accusations fell on deaf ears at city hall. In 1955 the city council, convinced that a housing shortage limited the city's ability to attract industry, demanded that the planning commission approve all requests to build multi-family housing. In accord with this resolution the zoning commission permitted the construction of apartments in two previously exclusive, single-family home districts. For homeowners in these neighborhoods the approval of apartments set an ominous precedent. As one homeowner put it,

this [the new apartment complex] is the opening wedge to increase the density ... A lot of it is conjecture I admit, but I feel this is the crack in the dike that will eventually cause a flood.[14]

In the more scenic, outlying areas, land use evolved in a different direction. Homeowners from northern Norwalk pointed out at public hearings that spacious subdivisions of single-family homes were the only appropriate land use for their hilly, "back country" districts. That point established, the residents argued for and obtained an increase in the minimum lot area required for new homes in their districts.[15] Following the change in the law, developers began building more expensive homes in the upgraded districts. Residents from the socially desirable shoreline districts also argued for increases in the minimum lot area. Impressed by the residents' resolve, the mayor of Norwalk supported the applications for upgrading. In his words,

The folks in this part of town like to think of their area as a village. They are jealous of this village atmosphere, and I am very jealous that they continue to have it. Unless we do bring about reasonable upgrading in this area, that village atmosphere cannot prevail much longer.[16]

In these cases wealthy homeowners succeeded in imposing their will on the local authorities. In their success they stand in stark contrast to the middle-income homeowners who failed to prevent the construction of multi-family housing in their neighborhoods.

Over time these policies affected the destinations of in-migrants to Norwalk. Decisions to prohibit the construction of everything but expensive housing in outlying districts attracted wealthy in-migrants to these areas while decisions to locate all eight of Norwalk's low-income housing projects in the downtown area drew poor in-migrants to the center city. Between 1960 and 1980 these selective migratory streams contributed to increased income inequality and racial segregation in Norwalk.[17]

The differences in the residential composition of local areas affect the way Norwalk residents identify with their neighborhoods. These attitudes show up in small, but revealing ways. At cocktail parties the residents of Rowayton, an exclusive shoreline area, when asked where they live, always respond by saying 'Rowayton' rather than 'Norwalk'. In addition to minimizing their association with Norwalk, the residents of the upper class enclaves usually ascribe a 'special' character to their place of residence. In contrast the residents of a middle- or lower-class area usually regard their neighborhood as a "mixed bag," containing all types of people and no special character.[18] By the 1970s Norwalk had become a collection of distinct neighborhoods held together by an overarching political system while Westport had evolved into a homogeneous upper-class community.

Westport: land-use conversion and control in a suburb

Conflict, fine-grained rules, and trilateral relational controls

Except for a commercial strip which bisects the town, land use in Westport consists almost entirely of single-family homes interspersed with woodland. The uniform pattern of land use has affected citizen participation in land-use planning. During periods of rapid growth when rumors of proposed real estate developments circulated in every section of the town, similarities in the threats posed by developments gradually convinced homeowners from different neighborhoods that they had a common interest in planning. The homeowners institutionalized this interest through a coalition of neighborhood associations which, beginning in 1965, lobbied for decisions favorable to their interests and ran homeowner candidates for seats on the planning and zoning commission. Since 1965 homeowner candidates have become commissioners with great regularity; in office they have wielded decisive influence in the formulation of local land-use policy.

The power of Westport's homeowners becomes apparent when the land-use authorities try to amend the zoning regulations to permit multi-family housing. On one occasion, in mid June, 1973, municipal authorities proposed an amendment and went so far as to solicit applications from developers. The homeowners' response to the commissioners' initiative took shape slowly. At first they evinced no interest in the apartment amendment. Few people attended the public hearings on the amendment, and the letters to the editor of the local newspaper concerned other issues. Then, in late June, approximately ten days before the representative town meeting was to vote on the amendment, the local newspaper ran a front-page article which speculated about the impact of apartments on the quality of life in Westport. The article touched off a burst of political activity. In the ten days between the publication of the article and the vote, petitions opposing the amendment circulated in two neighborhoods, 30 to 40 letters critical of the amendment appeared in the local press, and the 38 representatives to the town meeting received more than 1,500 phone calls from constituents who wanted them to vote against apartments.[19] In the week preceding the vote the leaders of the anti-apartment movement argued against the amendment in public statements, held two mass meetings with their supporters, and charged a commission member with a conflict of interest. The political commotion ended abruptly when the representatives to the town meeting voted unanimously to prohibit the construction of apartments in Westport. The day after the vote to reject the amendment, the hastily formed coalition fell apart, the leaders returned to their private affairs, and the rank and file lost interest in the issue.[20]

With a mandate to maintain residential exclusivity, Westport's land-use authorities have created a more elaborate and fine-grained set of rules about land use. The growing scarcity of undeveloped land encouraged the adoption of more fine-grained rules. With declines in the size of the remaining tracts of undeveloped land, the buffer zones between new developments and adjacent land users shrank, and under these conditions even small features of a proposed development became a source of disturbances. To prevent these interferences, the land-use authorities have increased their regulation of the minor aspects of developments. The increased concern for detail shows up in two ways. First, the selectmen have established a new procedure, the site plan review, and a new commission, the architectural review board, to evaluate the design of proposed developments. Secondly, the planning and zoning commissioners have adopted more elaborate rules. They have refined their list of permitted uses, encouraged developers to present more elaborate plans for review, and added extra steps to the process of review, all in an attempt to regulate the detail of proposed developments. For example, in revising their list of permitted uses, the commissioners took a provision which permitted

410.2 Customary home occupations including professional or commercial offices, and home industries or service occupations carried out by a resident of the premises.

and replaced it with two provisions.

9.21 Doctor, dentist, and real estate offices.
9.22 The restoration and sale of antiques, commercial gardens, and private day care centers (not to exceed fifteen children).[21]

The new provisions narrowed the definitions of permitted occupations and prohibited other occupations entirely. At the same time the commission considered and eventually rejected a provision which would have required lawyers, realtors and other professionals to obtain licenses to practice their occupations in their homes. The commissioners also considered adopting rules for buffering and screening which would have regulated landscaping down to the caliper of the trees in the yard. They never formally proposed the adoption of the landscaping rules because homeowners objected to them. As one resident put it in a question to a commissioner,

How can you do that? Are you going to tell me what I can plant in my own front yard?[22]

Attempts to control detail in commercial development met with more popular approval. An editorial in the Westport *News* provides a representative sampling of local opinion.

Nearly everywhere you go these days, it seems there is a Burger King restaurant selling hamburgers and milkshakes. And nearly every Burger King has the characteristic red trim, and the company name in bright orange letters. Now Westport too has a Burger King. But the Westport version, which opened last week, is different. A testament to the persistence of two town planning groups, the local restaurant... has a more subdued red trim on its roof, no bright orange letters and landscaping instead of parking in front.[23]

Despite the creation of more discriminating rules, changes in the characteristics of undeveloped land have made it more difficult to control land use through the application of rules. An increasing proportion of the undeveloped tracts of land contain topography which make development difficult, if not impossible. As one commissioner has remarked, "all the land we get now is troubled land. Most everything that is decent is gone."[24] To build on these properties, developers have to 'bend' the rules. For example, a developer with a lien to purchase a 35-acre tract of undeveloped land found that more than 20 acres of the land was unsuitable for building. With the land under a two-acre minimum lot area requirement, the developer could only build on the remaining 15 acres of land; his profits would be limited to whatever he could make from the seven houses he could put on the land. The developer could increase the number of houses, and his profits, through a plan which located 17 homes on the 15 acres of good land and satisfied the two acre requirement by creating a corporation, composed of the 17 homeowners, which would own the entire 35-acre tract of land.[25] With the zoning commission's blessing, the developer had devised a new type of development, different in both its legal form and physical arrangement from a standard subdivision of single-family homes. Almost every effort to build on 'troubled' land generates plans whose approval requires a departure from the simple rules which guided commission actions during the 1950s and 1960s.

Other departures from simple, exclusionary rules occurred after the intervention of a third party in conflicts between homeowners and developers. Most of these conflicts concerned commercial land uses. The controversies had their origins in the widespread desire of corporate executives to move their offices out of New York City. Local officials did not discourage corporate relocations because the property taxes on the new offices represented a new source of revenue at a time when increments in revenue from a traditional source, the construction of single-family homes, were declining.[26] While local politicians were ambivalent about office construction, most homeowners opposed it out of a concern that the offices would trigger a process of land-use conversion which would adversely affect property values in Westport. These disputes usually involved only those homeowners living near the site for development, but, when the site was centrally located, controversy engulfed the entire community.

Controversies occur more frequently in Westport (see table 8) and involve somewhat different contestants than they do in rural–urban fringe communities. As in fringe communities, homeowners confront developers, but suburban homeowners are wealthier and better organized than their counterparts in fringe areas, so well-organized homeowners face well-financed developers. Each organization spends liberally for legal counsel and technical expertise in presenting their case to local officials and, if necessary, before judges in the state courts. The expense, delay, and aggravation experienced by parties to these conflicts comes across in a statement by a Westport zoning commissioner (Tarrant, 1976:22).

I took this job because I wanted to do something for the town. Of course I receive no pay for it. Up to a point, I was able to stand the abuse I had to take at meetings and the abusive phone calls at all hours of the night from people who did not like a decision or people who suspected that there would be a decision which they would not like. But it's the lawyers who have made it too much to take. No matter how routine a case may seem when it starts out, you can always be sure that – before very long – there will be at least two groups of contending parties, fully represented by expensive counsel. And – no matter how the decision goes – you can be sure that the side that does not win will take it to court, and will keep it in court right up through the full extent of the possibilities.

In the midst of another controversy several years later a Westport lawyer registered the same complaint.

In any other town this [issue] would be cut and dried. Here we have battles and go to court on every little dispute. The judge over in Bridgeport said he was going to have to open up a special Westport branch. We fight about everything.[27]

The data in table 8 offer proof for the lawyer's point. Half of the Westport commission's 1979 actions led to litigation in the state courts. To avoid litigation, interested parties have recently begun to negotiate with one another. Developers consulted with nearby homeowners about drainage patterns in a neighborhood before they drew up a plan of development.[28] In another instance after nine years of acrimony involving two lawsuits, a developer, the homeowners, and the commissioners began to negotiate directly with one another. The commissioners and the developer had some difficulty negotiating with a "loose knit" group of homeowners, but they persisted until the three groups agreed upon a residential use for the land.[29] In a third instance neighboring homeowners withdrew their suit against a proposed mobile-home park when the developer "agreed to buy their homes at 5 percent more than market value if they could not get a better price when they put their homes up for sale."[30] In a final instance a developer came to the commission with four alternative plans for developing a tract of land and invited the commissioners to indicate their preference before he prepared a formal plan.

A modified form of this last procedure has become commonplace in recent years. The builder consults with the town planner before he submits a plan for development. When the planner thinks that a proposed development would be unacceptable to the commission, he advises against an application. If approval appears possible, the planner and the developer consider the layouts which the development could take without disrupting the lives of nearby homeowners. Through sometimes lengthy negotiations the planner and developer 'fit' the development into the surrounding pattern of land use. On occasion the developer and the commissioners negotiate a permissible use for the land through a series of proposals. The commission rejects the first proposal; the developer discusses the rejected plan with citizens and town officials, modifies the proposal, and resubmits it to the commission. On the second or third try the commission often approves the project.

The process of negotiation often continues after the commission has approved a project. Between 1960 and 1970 the percentage of conditional approvals increased from 13 percent to 54 percent of all applications.[31] These actions make a project's approval contingent on specific changes which the developer agrees to make. If the developer fails to make the changes, the commission can withdraw its approval of the project. In effect conditional approvals extend the period of negotiation between the developer and the commission into the period of construction.

The increase in the number of commissions which review projects, the frequent denial and resubmission of projects, and the conditional approvals all lengthen the regulatory process. These changes in the review process embed a single action, such as the submission of a project proposal, in a sequence of social actions. This change should increase the incidence of cooperative behavior among developers. Because the opponents of development can intervene again and again in decisive ways in the lengthy process of reviewing a land-use change, the shadow of the future, in the form of a denied application, looms large in most developers' minds. To reduce the chances of a denial, developers make overtures to the commissioners and in some cases to interested homeowners.

If controversies persist and the contending parties do not negotiate with one another, third parties begin to propose plans. For example, after almost a decade of bitter controversy over apartment construction, the planning and zoning commission produced a plan which permitted the construction of a limited number of apartments for the elderly. In another instance in the late 1970s, land-use authorities produced a plan designed to provide multi-family housing and prevent further deterioration in an already serious traffic problem. After much controversy developers had succeeded in constructing a string of office buildings along Route 2 in the mid 1970s. With the completion of the offices traffic on Route 2 worsened. To prevent further deterioration in traffic conditions, the commission declared a moratorium on development along Route 2 and began to reassess its regulations for the area.[32] To this end the commissioners walked the land, consulted with the neighboring landowners, and then decided to rezone the area for multi-family housing. The new regulations established a zone for multi-family housing along Route 2 and the western boundary of the town (the cross-hatched area in figure 8). Because apartments generate fewer automobile trips than do offices, the new plan lessened the potential for congestion on the roads, and, because the site was adjacent to multi-family housing in the neighboring city, it seemed to be a more appropriate site for multi-family housing than other locations in Westport. After the landowners commented on the plan, the planners revised it, and the commissioners voted to accept it.

These procedures differ from the procedures used in fringe communities. In fringe areas a developer brings a plan to the commission, and the commissioners either accept it or reject it. In Westport the commissioners develop plans after consulting with all of the interested parties. The differences between the two procedures suggest that, as an affluent suburb becomes more built-up, land-use planning shifts away from a system in which developers have the initiative and simple rules guide the commis-

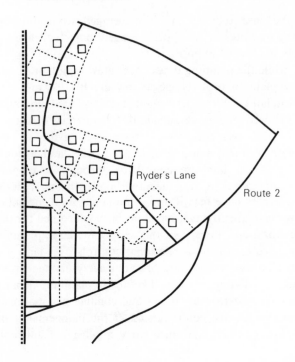

::::::::: Town boundary
---------- Property boundary
☐ Single-family home

Figure 8 *The Ryder's Lane neighborhood*

sioners, to a system in which planners sometimes have the initiative and flexible rules guide the commissioners in the processing of applications.

Before the planners can settle on a plan which will minimize conflict, they have to conduct studies to evaluate the relative merits of alternative plans. The time required to conduct the studies lengthens the planning process to the point where it irritates local residents. As the *News* put it in the headline of a 1976 article on land-use planning, "Studies and more studies block progress in Westport."[33] The proliferation of studies proved to be a boon for professional planners. The execution of some studies, the evaluation of other studies, and the development of plans which addressed controversial issues required an increasing number of planners in Westport. By 1978 the planning department had grown to eight fulltime members. The planning and zoning commissioners shared in the increased work load. While commission meetings in the other case study communities averaged two to three hours in length, the evening meetings in Westport averaged more than five hours in length and usually adjourned after 1 a.m.[34]

Paradoxically, while the planning department grew rapidly in size, citizen interest in land-use planning probably began to wane. By 1977 only 5 percent of the privately held land in Westport remained undeveloped, and real estate development had slowed to a crawl outside the commercial districts. Large numbers of Westport residents found themselves living in built-up neighborhoods with a sound housing stock and little land available for development.[35] Significant land-use conversion through development or deterioration does not occur in these neighborhoods. In the Ryder's Lane subdivision homeowners have few, if any, complaints about neighborhood conditions. The most frequently mentioned problem concerned the depredations of the neighborhoods' dogs.[36] In this setting the large planning staff testifies to the reliance on trilateral relational controls over land use. In a context in which land-use changes are few, but every change provokes a prolonged dispute, mediating entities, like town planning departments, become important. They carry out studies and conduct negotiations which attempt to prevent or resolve controversies. If the planners fail in these attempts, the disputes go to another third party, a judge in a state court, for resolution.

Accessory apartments and the persistence of bilateral relational controls

While Westport's fine-grained legal controls purport to control all types of land-use changes, some changes such as the remodelling of homes to accommodate accessory apartments remain beyond the reach of the law. A sharp drop in average household size, from 3.2 to 2.8 persons between 1970 and 1980, begins to explain the widespread remodelling of homes. Because house size remained constant, the decline in household size signalled an increase in the number of small households living in large houses. To defray the costs of maintaining large homes, some of these homeowners converted the vacant space in their homes into accessory apartments. By 1978 approximately 1,000 to 1,200 of the 6,500 single-family homes in Westport had an illegal accessory apartment on the premises.[37] In most cases the second household at an address consisted of one or two persons residing in one-, two-, or three-room apartments in poolhouses, over garages, or in the wings of large houses. The rents for advertised in-house apartments in Westpoint averaged between $200 and $300 per month during the 1975 to 1977 period.[38] At these prices low- to middle-income individuals could afford to rent the apartments. Given the adamant opposition to low- and middle-income multi-family housing, the relative absence of opposition to in-house apartments comes as a surprise. Some Westport residents welcomed the trend. In their opinion the creation of accessory apartments would resolve a longstanding problem by providing low-income housing without damaging the residential ambiance of the community. A prominent Westport resident put it neatly. "I would love to see Westport keep beautiful houses as they are on the outside but rearrange them on the inside."[39]

The physical layout of Westport's subdivisions probably contributes to the widespread acceptance of illegal apartments. The considerable distance between homes in one and two acre subdivisions minimizes the disturbances which the extra households cause nearby landowners, so neighbors rarely have cause to complain about apartment dwellers. What is more, the houses are often set so far back from the road that a passerby such as a zoning enforcement officer cannot determine which houses have in-house apartments and which houses do not. Under these conditions a local officer of the League of Women Voters advised homeowners to ignore the laws prohibiting accessory apartments. In her words accessory apartments are "illegal, but not very illegal."[40]

Officials will only enforce the law in cases in which neighbors complain about the presence of an illegal apartment in a home. Efforts at enforcement have occurred infrequently. The Westport *News* described the pattern.

After about a dozen complaints, few homeowners seemed willing to come forward to complain about a neighbor's apartment. The reluctance to do so seems related to the 'touchy' question of whether residents should be called upon to spy on their neighbors.[41]

The circumstances surrounding a complaint in the Ryder's Lane area illustrate how face to face relationships between neighbors contribute to a reluctance to complain to town officials about accessory apartments. In this instance a homeowner created an accessory apartment in 1972. After complaining to the homeowner about the apartment, a neighbor filed a complaint with the zoning enforcement officer who then inspected the apartment and issued a cease and desist order. Several months later the homeowner sold the house to a young couple who continued to rent out the apartment. The neighbor, in part because he knows that the former owner told the couple that they could rent out the apartment, seems reluctant to revive his complaint. After four years of existence through two owners and one half-hearted attempt to eliminate it, the apartment seems "less illegal" and more tolerable to the neighbor.[42] When activity at the apartment bothers the neighbor, he complains to the couple and they try to accommodate him. In this situation relational controls appear to offer an effective means of control. Discussions between homeowners or between the homeowner and the tenant over noise, parking, and the number of names on a mailbox reduce the visibility of the apartment dwellers and diminish the disturbances which they cause nearby homeowners.[43]

Norwalk: land-use conversion and control in a satellite city

The political context of developer dominance

Countervailing trends characterized the construction of new housing in Norwalk during the 1970s. While a growing scarcity of undeveloped land caused a decline in the construction of single-family homes during the 1970s, building patterns in the surrounding suburbs stimulated an increase in the construction of multi-family housing in Norwalk. By permitting the construction of offices and prohibiting the construction of multi-family housing, suburban officials created jobs for low-income workers and forced them to look elsewhere for housing. In effect these policies created a demand for housing and channeled it toward the only community in the region which permitted sizable amounts of attached housing. As one condominium owner put it, "Norwalk is a vacuum into which things are flowing at a heady pace."[44].

Norwalk residents reacted to the construction of multi-family housing in different ways in different neighborhoods. While the residents of the more exclusive areas worried about the effects of multi-family housing on the residential atmosphere, their counterparts in more densely populated neighborhoods showed little concern because they anticipated that the new units would raise the value of their homes. These differences in interest limited the occasions when the residents of different neighborhoods made common cause before the land-use authorities.

Even when homeowners in different neighborhoods shared a common interest, coalitions across neighborhoods did not develop. For example, in 1970 when the planners considered the readoption of a provision which would permit the construction of apartments and condominium complexes in Norwalk, citizens showed little interest. When developers submitted plans to build under this provision, the residents reacted differently. The first four proposals to build attached housing under this provision elicited vigorous opposition from nearby homeowners, and in each instance the homeowners carried the case to the state courts and lost on the grounds that the newly adopted provision permitted the proposed development. Recently the prospect of a legal battle persuaded a developer and a homeowner group to negotiate a plan of development agreeable to both parties.[45] Aside from this case homeowners have exercised little influence over the construction of attached housing in Norwalk. Their limited influence stems in large part from the episodic, uncoordinated way in which they express their interests.

The divisions among Norwalk's residents encourage divisions among its commissioners. The low level of citizen interest in general issues of planning and zoning makes it difficult for the commissioners to use their record in office to build a political following among Norwalk residents, so the commissioners have few incentives to create a coherent program of land-use control. Without a program to support or oppose, the commission has no factions; rather it is a collection of individuals with special interests in planning and zoning issues. Several commissioners have a special interest in one issue, but they show little interest in other issues. Some commissioners take strong positions on issues which concern their neighborhood but show little interest in similar issues concerning other neighborhoods. Other commissioners juggle the public interest and their private interests in real estate. Judging from the poor attendance records of some commissioners, they have little interest in any of the proceedings.[46] This mix of interests reduces the likelihood that the commissioners will establish a coherent program of land-use control.

In the absence of any unifying political order the commission plans in piecemeal fashion. Because the commissioners have few incentives to put in the 'thousands' of hours of extra work required to reform the zoning law, they have never attempted to update the 1929 law. Changes in the law occur only after a developer has made a particularly abusive but legal use of his land. For example, until 1978 the law allowed developers to place multi-unit structures anywhere on a lot provided that the buildings did not cover more than 25 percent of the land area. In building an apartment complex on lands whose eastern boundary was the Westport–Norwalk town line, a developer complied with the 25 percent limitation, but, in hopes of capitalizing on his location along the border of a prestigious residential community, he constructed the buildings so that they extended right up to the Westport town line. With this location the developer was able to put an access road through to a Westport subdivision road and claim a Westport address. Belatedly the Westport planners protested the developer's site plan, and, in response to this protest, the commissioners pushed through a regulation requiring that multi-unit structures be set back 80 feet from the property line.[47] In this manner the law undergoes revision. After public outcry over an abusive land use, the commissioners close the loophole which permitted the abuse.

The absence of a sense of mission makes individual commissioners especially vulnerable to outside attempts to influence them. Mayors have influenced commissioners by taking public stands on issues. On occasion outpourings of public sentiment influence the commissioners. More frequently, developers exert influence over the commission. Developers are most likely to win a favorable decision when they hire an influential Norwalk politician to represent them before the commission. Working with the vague, almost uninterpretable provisions of an antiquated law, the politician almost always convinces the commissioners that the developers' plans do not clearly violate the law. In this manner developers, their lawyers, and the commissioners achieve, over time, an understanding about acceptable and unacceptable land uses. In other words norms about land use emerge; developers submit proposals which do not violate the norms, and the commissioners cooperate by approving the projects.[48] These norms emerge in an iterative fashion as the same developers and lawyers submit a series of proposals to a commission whose composition changes very little. The small number of denied applications (see table 8) indicates how permissive the commissioners are and how well the developers have learned the norms which they must observe to obtain approval for their projects. Some citizens suspect that the norms involve not only land-use practices but collusive, sometimes corrupt arrangements between developers and commissioners.[49]

The events surrounding the approval of the Hidden Lake condominiums on Putney Avenue (see figure 9) illustrate the pattern of regulation. Developers from Long Island presented the commission with plans for developing Hidden Lake in 1977. To protect themselves from idiosyncratic practices in local land-use control, the developers hired an influential Norwalk lawyer to represent them before the commission. Opposition to the proposed development came primarily from the residents of Maplewood, a nearby condominium development. When they first heard about the Hidden Lake proposal, Maplewood residents expressed surprise, having been led to believe by their realtor that the woods north of Putney Avenue would not be developed in the immediate future. The fears of the Maplewood residents focused on the prospect of a 'condo ghetto' developing along Putney Avenue. One resident predicted that "this place will look like the older part of Brooklyn in ten years."[50] In arguing against the proposed development, the opponents focused on the traffic which the new development would generate around the two schools at the head of Putney Avenue. Parents worried about heavy traffic during the school year when their children

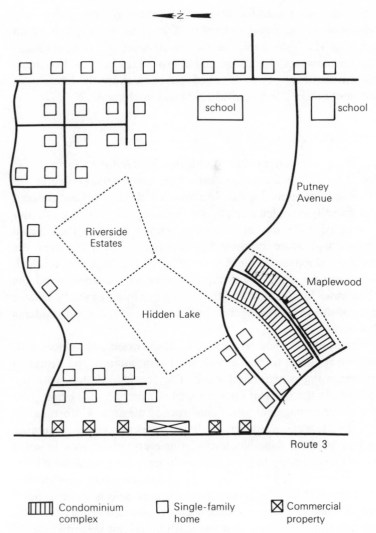

Figure 9 *The Putney Avenue neighborhood*

walked up and down Putney Avenue on their way to and from the schools. The parents maintained that the developer's report on traffic problems ignored the dangers associated with an increase in traffic during the school year. After considerable discussion the commissioners decided to resolve the issue by having the city traffic department conduct an independent study of traffic on Putney Avenue. Instead of conducting its survey on a weekday during the school year, the traffic department conducted the survey on a holiday weekend when, according to local residents, traffic is very light. With data documenting the light traffic on Putney Avenue, the commissioners dismissed the homeowners' objections and approved the project. For many homeowners this sequence of events raised questions about the integrity of traffic department officials and land-use planners in Norwalk.[51]

Defects in construction and trilateral relational controls

The susceptibility of the commission to influence by developers insures that the work of the city's planners focuses to an extraordinary degree on problems in already developed areas. In most case these problems concern the quality of recently completed roads and buildings. The absence of strict regulation, coupled with the developers' attempts to raise their profit margins on middle-income housing by "cutting corners," insures the construction of developments with defects. After the buildings are occupied, the defects become the focus of disputes between the occupants and the developer. The bases for conflicts and the strategies which eventually resolve them are evident in the history of a dispute between Maplewood residents and their builder.

In 1976, with approximately 40 percent of Maplewood's units occupied, the newly arrived residents formed a residential association in an attempt to monitor the remaining construction work. They concluded that, with the exception of leaks in the roofs of approximately 25 percent of the units, the developer had done a competent job of constructing the units. Unfortunately the quality of the site work was poor. Drainage problems existed. A number of residents had water in their basements after every rain storm. In some places the grass turned brown because the developer did not put down a layer of topsoil before he put down the sod. When an independent construction consultant examined the subdivision road, two more defects came to light. The builder had failed to put gravel beneath the road in some places, and he had skimped on asphalt so much that the hardtop did not reach the legally mandated thickness for public roads.

The officers of the residential association took these complaints to the planning and zoning commission and tried to get the commission to hold up the release of the $500,000 construction bond posted by the developer. In the words of one resident, the commissioners seemed 'uninterested' in the residents' complaints and tried to mollify them with assurances that "they would get back to them [the residents] later." Shortly thereafter the commission released $230,000 of the developer's bond. Irate at the treatment accorded them by the commission and the developer, Maplewood residents began to attend public hearings on the builder's plan for another development in Norwalk. At these meetings they recounted their problems with the developer and recommended that public officials deny him permission to build again in Norwalk. Finally, in response to persistent complaints by Maplewood residents, the commissioners agreed to inspect the development in the company of the developer and the residents.

According to stories recounted by the residents for several weeks after the inspection, incidents during the inspection cast doubt on several commissioners' impartiality; at one point a commissioner pointed towards the commissioners who had walked ahead and said to the citizens present, "they're all on the take." According to several residents some commissioners behaved accordingly. Whenever a resident pointed out and began to describe a faulty drainage system, two or three commissioners would move off in another direction and begin praising other aspects of the development. These incidents, coupled with the acquisition of three Maplewood units by the chairman of the planning and zoning commission, confirmed the residents' suspicions that the developer had 'bought' the commission. When the chairman purchased a unit and gave it to his son, the residents, not to be outdone by the developer in the exercise of influence, elected the chairman's son head of the residential association in an attempt to increase their influence with the commission.[52]

The city was reluctant to call the bond and make the repairs at Maplewood. According to the city planning director,

The city could call the bond, but we'd only do that as a last resort. We're not up to that point yet, and we're not rushing Mr. Danforth [the developer]...Usually deciding to call the bond involves a judgment of degree.[53]

After a year of trying to apply pressure on the developer through the planning and zoning commission, Maplewood residents tried a new strategy. They collected approximately $90,000 from the association's members for use in repairing roofs and doing drainage work around the units with flooded basements. The homeowners hoped to recover their costs through a suit which they had brought against the developer.

The conflicts which do not end up in court follow another path. If the homeowners apply enough political pressure, the planners threaten to withhold the developer's bond money until he does the repair work. These threats bring the developer, the planners, and the homeowners together to bargain about the extent of the repair work. When the developer makes the repairs, he does so grudgingly. With the intention of doing just enough work to get the bond money, the developer digs makeshift drainage ditches, lays sod on minimal layers of topsoil, and uses cheap patching material on the roads. In the words of one planner, things get done "right, the wrong way."[54] The accommodations which end the dispute come from face to face negotiations between an intermediary and the two contending parties.

Land-use conflicts between communities

When a wave of land-use conversion sweeps through an area, some communities succeed in establishing rule-based controls while other communities do not. The success of some communities contributes to the failure of others. Restrictive land-use regulations in the affluent, inner suburbs force the developers of low status, disruptive land uses such as dumps, gravel pits, and apartment complexes to locate on the periphery, and it compels younger, poorer households to rent housing in the same communities. Within the metropolitan core the exclusionary rules concentrate environmentally degrading activities in communities with poor, racially mixed populations. In effect the restrictive regulations compel those individuals and enterprises who oppose restrictive controls to locate in communities which have had the most difficulty establishing rule-based controls over land use. The redistribution of development interests towards emerging urban centers makes it more difficult to establish land-use controls in these places and easier to establish land-use controls in suburbs. While one community suffers from a lack of regulation, an adjacent community suffers from an excess of regulation. City residents complain about the lack of control over the developer who built their homes while suburban residents endure attempts to regulate the landscaping in their front yards.

The incidence of housing and neighborhood problems across the two communities reflects the differences in conversion and control. In the Putney Avenue area in Norwalk 33 percent of the homeowners complained about structural defects in their homes, and 60 percent complained about disruptive land uses nearby. In contrast only 6 percent of the homeowners in the Ryder's lane area of Westport complained about structural defects, and only 3 percent complained about disruptive land uses in the neighborhood. These environmental differences make it easy for suburban homeowners to associate the neighboring city with other urban problems. As one Westport homeowner put it,

If it were my desire to live in a so called 'balanced' community then I would move to a Norwalk, Stamford, or New Rochelle where strip slums abound along major thoroughfares and office buildings compete with apartments, and the tempo of life is spiced by the din of traffic and the excitement of possible muggings and robberies.[55]

These attitudes make Westport residents reluctant to visit nearby cities. This insular pattern of activity seems strange to newcomers to the Connecticut suburbs.

I'm from Ohio and there we thought nothing of driving 10 miles in either direction to go shopping. But here it is just not done. You don't go to those places, that's all.[56]

The city–suburb contrast becomes so salient in the minds of suburban homeowners that it begins to influence the way they think about land-use conflicts in their community. Conflicts between homeowners and developers take on overtones of conflicts between communities. Developers base their operations on cities because only cities have a pool of construction workers and sites to store construction equipment. As a result every developer who works in the suburbs is, in the eyes of the residents, an 'outside' developer who has come to their community to make money at their expense.

Differences in opinions about regional development projects reinforce the suburbanites' view of the city as an "engine of growth" whose residents show excessive dedication to profit-making activities. For example, the construction of Route 7, a limited access highway, promised to alleviate traffic jams and reinvigorate the commercial real estate markets in Danbury and Norwalk. Both city and suburban residents anticipated these impacts, but they drew opposite conclusions about the project's desirability. Suburban residents opposed it; city residents supported it. In another instance Westport and Norwalk officials disagreed about a plan which would have permitted Norwalk to dispose of its garbage through a Westport transfer station. Under this plan Norwalk garbage trucks would have transported their garbage to a Westport site where it would have been transferred to larger trucks for the trip to the recycling plant in Bridgeport. In Westport 1,000 residents signed a petition opposing the plan. Westport's selectmen rejected the plan because the town would not receive any compensation for the disturbances and damage to roads which the garbage trucks would cause.[57]

Public officials' incentives to cooperate on regional projects like garbage disposal decline with the region's growth rate. The gains and losses to a community from a regional project are often clear. Westport officials could envision the environmental degradation which would occur if Norwalk shipped its garbage through Westport, and they could not imagine any way in which Norwalk officials could repay them for these costs. The one other outstanding issue between the two towns involved the demand by Norwalk officials that Westport permit the construction of low-income housing within its borders. These two issues did not provide the basis for quid pro quo arrangements, and with few other regional sewer and highways projects in the planning stages the opportunities for similar arrangements on other projects did not appear good. The decline in the number of regional projects which required cooperation between communities had reduced the opportunities for log rolling, for giving on one project in order to get on another project. Under these conditions when planners proposed a project which offered benefits to some but not to all towns, officials in the latter towns emphasized the project's immediate costs and discounted the value of the political capital which they could accumulate by cooperating on the project. As a result the political authorities usually disagreed, and conflicts occurred. Without a regional government to mediate conflicts, these disputes ended up in the courts where they remained unresolved for years.

While the disputes over regional projects did not improve relations between local governments, the primary points of conflict concerned the refusal of suburban communities to permit the construction of low-income housing. Suburban land-use planning insured that poor in-migrants, whose contributions in taxes would not cover their costs in public services, would settle in Norwalk. The inequities of this situation prompted one Norwalk politician to remark that,

It's got to the point where all the regional solutions come from Norwalk and all the regional problems come from places like Westport... They [Westport residents] have this snobbish attitude that Norwalk should provide all of the services, and they should have all the clean air and nice lawns. It's not fair.

We get revenue sharing money, and we have to spend it on police pensions and housing for the elderly while they get to spend it on tennis courts.[58]

Conflict over the issue marked the proceedings of the regional planning commissions during the 1970s. Because suburban representatives outnumbered city representatives on the southwestern Connecticut commission, the suburban commissioners set the tone for the advisory opinions which the commission issued on proposals for real estate development in the area. On several occasions in the late 1970s the suburban commissioners angered their urban counterparts by opposing proposals for development in Norwalk. Consistent with the restrictive land-use policies pursued by their constituents, the suburban representatives voted against revenue generating projects in Norwalk which, by virtue of their location, would have encouraged development in the suburbs.[59] Norwalk politicians attempted to use the regional planning commission for the New York metropolitan area to influence land-use decisions in the suburbs. When Westport applied for federal assistance in financing the purchase of a centrally located 32-acre tract of land for open space, Norwalk officials argued that Westport should be compelled to build low-income housing on the land. City officials have

attempted to block other Westport requests for federal funds, in one instance
to subsidize a local bus system, in another instance to renovate an elementary
school for use as the town hall.[60]

Although a high degree of economic inequality existed between Norwalk
and its neighbors in the 1950s and 1960s, attempts by city politicians to
achieve more equity did not begin until 1975. Changing tolerance for these
inequalities (Hirschman, 1973) probably explains the slow resort to protest.
On several occasions in the 1940s during debates over land use, Norwalk
residents pointed out that their community competed with the surrounding
suburbs in attempting to attract young households moving out of New York
City.[61] These comments were not hostile in tone; they suggested that the
competition between communities was a benign one in which all communities
would benefit to varying degrees. By the 1970s the selective nature of
the migratory streams had become clearer, and the assumptions about the
benign nature of the competition had become more questionable. The
surrounding suburbs received the wealthiest migrants while the city received
the middle and lower-income migrants. The slowdown in residential
development during the 1970s made it unlikely that future development
would correct these inequities. By implication Norwalk's disadvantages in
the present would remain its disadvantages in the future. Recognition of this
situation prompted the protests by Norwalk's leaders. The subsequent
conflicts went on until a third party, either in the state courts or the federal
government, ruled on the merits of the communities' contentions.

Urban land use, conflict, and trilateral relational controls

Core community planning requires a different orientation from land-use
planners. In this setting the problem of control becomes increasingly one of
managing conflict. Comparisons of land-use planning in core and periphery
communities establish that fewer projects are proposed for core communities
and that a much higher proportion of these projects provide occasions for
conflict both within and between communities. The increase in density
provokes more conflict. Inequalities grow, and people become more
intolerant of them. In this setting a new form of land-use control emerges,
one which relies on third parties to play an active role in adjudicating the
claims of the contending parties.

The renewed reliance on relational controls in urban communities reflects
changes in relations between the interested parties. The emergence of a
multi-staged regulatory process in the affluent suburb creates continuing
relationships and therefore incentives to cooperate among the actors in land-

use planning. The shadow of future conflicts between the same developers and commissioners over other proposals provides the developer with additional incentives for cooperative action. These relational controls operate to a greater extent in the affluent suburb than they do in the satellite city. In the city the developers' dominance restricts the range of situations in which relational controls come into play. Because developers do not anticipate the denial of their projects, they feel no need to negotiate with homeowners or commissioners. Only when homeowners apply persistent pressure on issues of shoddy construction will planners negotiate with a developer in an attempt to mollify the homeowners. These intercommunity differences point out the restraining effects which inequalities of power have on the use of relational controls to control urban land use.

Differences in the balance of power between contending groups also account for differences between cities and suburbs in the substance of land-use controversies. In the suburb conflicts focus on the potential disruptions of proposed developments. The preoccupation with potential problems offers indirect testimony to the efficacy of the residents' earlier attempts to control land use. Most Westport residents like the present pattern of land use, so their attention focuses on threats to the pattern. In the satellite city conflicts concern problems created by shoddy, city-approved construction as well as problems posed by projected development. The focus on existing as well as potential problems reflects the developers' dominance of the planning process and the lack of control which the city has over the use of land within its borders.

Third parties in urban communities have more influence over the incidence and duration of conflicts than they do over substantive outcomes. In both cities and suburbs planners try to induce the different interest groups to adopt flexible positions which presage compromise between the contending parties and an end to a dispute. While planners assume a mediating role, they are not impartial referees. They do not adjudicate conflicts, rather they facilitate conflict resolution by providing the conflicting parties with estimates of what they can expect to get in a settlement. In suburbs the planner will advise a developer as to what the commission will or will not accept. In cities planners may advise homeowners on what they can expect to get in repairs from a developer accused of shoddy construction. In this sense planners broker solutions to conflicts. The solutions reflect the prevailing balance of power in local land-use politics rather than the impartial hand of a third party. The same observations apply to a lesser degree to conflicts which are resolved in the courts. The strength of the appellant's case almost always depends on the clarity and completeness of the local land-use law. In

Norwalk citizens bring most of the cases, the law is generally permissive, and citizens lose most cases. In Westport developers bring most of the cases; the law is restrictive, and developers lose most cases. Viewed in this light, the rise of third parties to prominence in urban land-use planning represents an attempt at conflict management which does not produce major changes in the substantive outcomes of conflicts.

7 Assessments and applications

In the maze of ethnographic detail presented in chapters 4, 5, and 6, the illustrative purpose of the case studies tends to get lost. Obviously the case studies do not provide a neat illustration of the theory outlined in chapter 2, but in their completeness they suggest both the theory's potential and its limitations. This chapter elaborates on these suggestions. It uses the case studies to evaluate growth-machine theory and the accompanying analyses of interest-group interactions. It also discusses the theory's usefulness for explaining patterns of land-use planning outside the northeastern United States. The final section of the chapter traces out two policy implications, one for low-income housing and another for community control of developers.

Growth machines in the four communities

The case studies of land-use planning provide an opportunity for testing the growth-machine model of local politics. Molotch (1976) argued that cities can be described as growth machines run by land-based elites for their own economic advantage. Because land-use planning prepares the ground for economic growth, growth coalitions should play an important role in local land-use planning. According to Molotch's model, the coalitions should take a particular form and exercise a certain amount of influence in land-use politics. If the growth coalitions present in the four case-study communities conform to these expectations, this research should provide a partial confirmation of growth-machine theory.

The results of this test should supplement the findings from a series of earlier tests of growth-machine theory (Lyon et al., 1981; Maurer and Christenson, 1982; Krannich and Humphrey, 1983; McGranahan, 1984) which either supported or specified the theory. The earlier tests have provided a welcome indication of the model's validity, but their reliance on data gathered through mail surveys limits what they can say about growth machines. As Molotch clearly indicates (1976:311), elite coalitions are variable entities. They pursue flexible strategies to gain their ends and change in form when the issues change. This dynamic dimension in land-use politics is difficult to capture in mail surveys of one or two community leaders at a single point in time. Modifications over time in a coalition's members and in its strategy for dealing with other interest groups are unlikely to show up in this type of analysis. The level of historical detail available in the case studies makes it possible to investigate these aspects of growth-machine theory.

A review of the growth machines in rural, rural–urban fringe, and suburban communities suggests that they differ in make-up and operation from the standard outlined by Molotch. In rural communities most real estate developments are so small in scale that political coalitions, contrary to the expectations of the growth-machine model, do not play a significant role in the community's acceptance of change. Interactions between individual landowners, one of whom is the builder, explain the acceptance or opposition to a proposed change in land use. The same type of interactions account for variations in the acceptance of small changes in urban land uses such as the creation of an accessory apartment in a house. The absence of growth coalitions in these instances invites speculation about the conditions which give rise to coalitions. One might argue that growth coalitions only become active when the contemplated development exceeds a certain size. Cities with their large markets and rural–urban fringe communities with their rapid growth rates would always have enough development to encourage the operation of growth coalitions. In rural communities and older suburbs where new construction occurs more infrequently, the operation of growth coalitions seems more problematic.

Growth coalitions were present in all four case-study communities, but they varied from community to community in their composition. Bankers, builders, realtors, newspaper editors, and local public officials made up urban growth coalitions. Farmers played an important role in rural and rural–urban fringe coalitions. As large landowners farmers are frequently party to real estate transactions which set the stage for major developments. Farmers also become developers. In most instances they build on a small scale, one or two houses a year, but, as the Woodridge Lake development in Goshen demonstrates, they can build on a large scale as well.

The ties which bind rural coalitions together are somewhat different from the ties which hold urban growth coalitions together. Farmers call on other economically interested landowners when they seek approval for projects, but they also call on relatives for political support. The relatives are often considerable in number. With ties to the community which may go back 100 years and low rates of residential mobility, farmers often have large numbers of relatives residing in the community. Kinship also provides the political basis for the disproportionately large number of farmers who become local public officials. In Goshen the first selectman was a part-time farmer; in New Milford the first selectman was a former farmer who had become a developer. In office these officials become an integral part of the local growth machine.

While the occupational make-up of growth coalitions varies from rural to urban communities, the political circumstances in which they operate varies between the satellite city and the other three case-study communities. In suburbs and to a lesser degree in rural and rural–urban fringe communities homeowners exercise considerable influence in local land-use planning. Homeowners fit uneasily into the growth-machine model. They form an interest group which on some occasions participates in land-use planning and in some places dominates the process politically, but they are too numerous to be considered an elite and have an anti-growth rather than a pro-growth ideology. Homeowner groups can be considered countervailing coalitions (Molotch and Logan, 1984) because they arise in response to proposed developments, but it is clear that suburban homeowners do not, as Molotch and Logan argue (1984), distinguish between local and outside developers in deciding whether or not to oppose a project. In the most affluent suburbs homeowners organize against virtually every development; in less affluent communities their response to a development depends on its anticipated impact on the value of their property, not on the characteristics of the developers.

Taken together, these observations about the activities of growth coalitions across communities suggest two conclusions. The case studies underscore the accuracy of Molotch's central idea, that communities give rise to growth coalitions which play an important role in local politics. The case studies also suggest more variability across communities in the make-up and political strength of growth coalitions than one would expect from the growth-machine model. As discussed earlier, the make-up of rural and rural–urban fringe growth coalitions varies in intelligible ways from their urban counterparts. More significantly, growth coalitions encounter varying levels of opposition across the four communities. In the satellite city, growth coalitions dominate the land-use planning process just as the model would predict. In the other three communities the opposition to development was significant enough to bring about changes in the legal controls over real estate development. These observations suggest that a more complete explanation of the patterns in local politics requires, in addition to analyses of how growth coalitions operate, analyses of how growth coalitions interact with other interest groups. To this end chapter 2 argued that the degree of cooperation or conflict among the parties interested in land-use changes in a locality affects the form of local land-use control. An assessment of this argument in light of the case studies follows.

Interactions between interested parties

Chapter 2 argued that credible explanations for patterns in land-use planning should link overarching structural variables with variables which conceptualize day to day political interactions between interested parties. The explanation developed here links structural variables such as changes in transportation or changes in a community's socio-economic composition to an interactional variable, the degree of conflict or cooperation among landowners. In concert the two types of variables should explain the reliance on relational controls in rural communities, the collapse of relational controls in rural–urban fringe areas, and the renewed reliance on relational controls in suburbs.

The case studies confirm the cross-sectional differences outlined above. In rural communities where land users are longterm acquaintances, land-use changes occur infrequently, and spillover effects are rare, informal agreements regulate most land uses. In rural–urban fringe communities where rapidly changing market conditions encourage noncooperative behavior among developers, governments create legally enforceable rules over land uses. In urban communities where intense use, close proximity, and a high degree of political mobilization make land-use conflict endemic, third parties mediate and in some cases decide the issues which divide the contending parties.

Taken together, the case studies suggest the presence of a developmental sequence in which, as communities become built-up, bilateral relational controls give way to rule-based controls which in turn evolve into trilateral relational controls. New controls do not completely displace old controls as communities develop. In rural–urban fringe communities rules replace informal controls in decision making about the conversion of large tracts of land, but informal controls continue to influence decisions about land uses within building lots. In urban communities third parties intervene in conversions which generate conflict, but noncontroversial conversions, such as the construction of a single-family home on a large lot or the creation of an accessory apartment in a home, continue to be handled through rule-based or bilateral relational controls.

Changes in these regulatory patterns occur incrementally. A new type of conversion occurs, the actors interested in conversion change, and the community responds to the changes with a regulatory innovation. The pre-existing regulatory procedures persist, but they apply to a narrower range of conversions. In this way as communities undergo real estate development, a series of regulatory accretions occur, and a multi-faceted regulatory regime emerges.

Because most of the evidence presented in the case studies comes from a collection of anecdotes gathered during interviews, the analyses of the impact of changes in interest-group interactions on land-use controls is more suggestive than conclusive. More convincing analyses will require improvements in the data. Anecdotes provide the appropriate type of data, descriptions of short sequences of social events, for assessing the argument. The ordering of events and the respondents' characterizations of them suggest the degree to which norms of reciprocity and tit-for-tat strategies govern interactions in a place. The problems concern the quantity and quality of the stories which people tell. To build data bases which permit tests of arguments like those presented here, we need sampling procedures which insure a representative set of stories, interview schedules which formalize the collection of stories, and measures of cooperation derived from the interactions described in the stories. Recent methodological work by historical sociologists (Abbott, 1983, 1984) begins to address these problems.

How robust are these results?

Given that the case studies all come from one metropolitan area, one might wonder about the theory's application to real estate development in other regions of the United States. Two problems complicate this task. The first problem concerns the timing of development in a place. While many suburbs in the Northeast experienced their most rapid development in the 1950s, suburbs in the South and West have experienced their most rapid development in the 1970s and 1980s. Communities undergoing development in the 1980s do so in a different context than did communities which developed in the 1940s and 1950s. For example, the diffusion of planning innovations from communities which develop early to communities which develop late should produce differences in the sequence of changes in land-use control. Negotiated planning techniques provide a case in point. Planners developed these techniques to deal with controversial construction projects in older metropolitan areas (Susskind, 1982). The techniques received much publicity, sometimes under the name of environmental mediation (Talbot, 1983; Bingham, 1985), and wide application (Butler and Myers, 1984) in peripheral communities where, according to the theory, we would not expect to see them applied. The favorable publicity surrounding the new techniques may have caused late-developing communities to leapfrog in the adoption of planning techniques, to go directly from bilateral to trilateral relational controls. In sum, late-developing communities both learn through the diffusion of ideas from older communities and develop in a political and social context which has been structured by development experiences in older communities (Molotch, personal communication). In this sense the timing of development may have an important effect on the way a community regulates itself.

A second variable, the organization of local government, would appear to belong in any comprehensive theory of land-use planning. Some analysts locate the cause for the crazy quilt pattern of land-use planning in the organization of local government. The report of the Rockefeller Task Force on Land Use and Urban Growth exemplifies this type of analysis (Reilly, 1973:212).

For any number of localities, proposing that decisions be based on consistent policies and plans seems laughably unrealistic. Many local governments operate under so many constraints that their power to make and implement consistent policy is extremely limited. Local governments must usually rely on archaic property tax systems for their funds. Many have tiny geographical jurisdictions which restrict both the range of their concern and their power to deal with regional development forces. Localities with small populations often can not afford to hire the skilled professionals needed to deal with complex development problems. Many governments have a tradition of passivity, of acting in a more or less custodial capacity; others enjoy their adhockery.

This description of land-use policymaking, along with other studies (Lorimer, 1979:124), suggests that the size of political jurisdictions shapes policy in important ways. Metropolitan areas in the United States vary from region to region in their degree of political fragmentation. The North Central and Northeastern regions have the most politically fragmented metropolitan areas (Zeigler and Brunn, 1980). The New York metropolitan area, for example, has 1,467 local governments while all of south Florida has only 22 local governments (Lemire, 1979:40; Wood, 1961). Because jurisdictions are small in politically fragmented areas, the market for land may not vary substantially within a jurisdiction. In this context a change in land-use conversion will affect the entire community; the large proportion of affected landowners in a jurisdiction increases the likelihood that the change in conversion will create enough political pressure to affect a change in controls. In larger jurisdictions such as the city of San Diego where market conditions vary from a built-up inner core to rural–urban fringe (Corso, 1983), changes in conversion in one area may not generate enough political pressure to bring about a change in controls. In these jurisdictions the link between processes of conversion and procedures of control should not be as direct as it is in smaller jurisdictions.

In addition to its effects on the variety of market conditions under regulation, the size of jurisdiction affects the level of political activity among its residents. A comparative study of subdivision approval in Dallas and Houston (Peiser, 1981) illustrates this effect. In the suburbs of Dallas local government is highly fragmented; each community has its own government, and citizen opposition to development varies across communities according to the socio-economic composition of local populations. In suburban Houston the political system is much less fragmented, citizen opposition to development is muted, and residential real estate development varies according to the location of city services. As Richard Peiser explains it, homeowner groups exert influence more effectively in the Dallas suburbs where they represent a major part of a political constituency than they do in Houston where a homeowner group represents only a small segment of a larger county electorate. The pattern of political activity outlined by Peiser accords with the logic of collective action. The greater ease of coalition formation among small numbers of people implies more collective action, *ceteris paribus*, in small jurisdictions than in large jurisdictions (Olson, 1982:33). By extension, politicians in larger jurisdictions should respond more slowly to homeowner discontent than do politicians in smaller jurisdictions.

Jurisdiction size has an indirect effect, through the heterogeneity of local populations, on the level of political activity. Governments with jurisdiction over large numbers of people tend to serve unusually heterogeneous constituencies. As the Norwalk case demonstrates, the racial, ethnic, and class differences within this type of constituency make it difficult for residents to build the coalitions necessary to challenge the developers' control of regulatory processes (Yates, 1977). The difficulties of coalition formation in turn contribute to political quiescence.

The argument about jurisdiction size has implications for regional differences in land-use planning. Because jurisdictions in southern suburban areas are generally larger, politicians in southern suburbs should respond more slowly to extensive land-use conversion than do politicians in northern suburbs. The lower levels of responsiveness should result in less restrictive controls in southern suburbs. What is more, by discouraging homeowner political action, centralization may suppress conflicts between homeowners and developers to the point where communities make less use of trilateral relational controls over land use.[1] These considerations cast the case studies in a new light. Because the case studies focus on communities outside center cities in a politically fragmented region, the governments under study have relatively small jurisdictions. They should therefore be more susceptible to homeowner domination than most local governments in the United States.

The foregoing arguments about the timing of development and the size of jurisdictions suggest both the limits and the potential of the theory outlined here. The arguments circumscribe but do not invalidate the theory. They make it clear that the theory applies most directly to communities in the older metropolitan areas. With the addition of the two variables discussed above, it should apply to communities throughout the United States.

Policy implications

The value of local land-use controls has been the subject of vigorous debate over the past 15 years. Advocates of local control point to its democratic value. Clearly local control encourages participatory democracy in ways in which no control, with its advantages for the wealthy, and state control, with its remote authorities, do not. One can also argue that those closest to the environment regulate it best (Weaver and Babcock, 1980; Lynch, 1981). Critics of comprehensive, top down planning (Goodman, 1971) and advocates of "neighborhood listening" approaches to planning (Goetze, 1983) make the same point. This assertion is only accurate if all those parties who 'know' the local environment have some representation in decision making about it. When one interested party such as homeowners in suburbs or developers in cities dominates land-use politics, the critics would appear to be accurate in their assertion that local decision making produces "parochial and protectionist policies without a sense of responsibility for the disadvantaged" (de Neufville, 1982:45).

The theory outlined and illustrated in the preceding chapters suggests why elite control produces so many land-use problems. By pointing to the close connections between changes in land-use conversion, changes in relations between landowners, and changes in land-use controls, the theory suggests that effective land-use planners either anticipate or respond quickly to changes in land use conversion in a community. When local business elites control land-use planning, they usually do not evidence the responsiveness which is the hallmark of effective planning in local government. Local business elites are sensitive to a small number of profit producing land-use conversions, but they have no incentives to acknowledge trends in land-use conversion which adversely affect less influential land users and no incentives to produce regulations which benefit or protect the large majority of land users in a community. Under these circumstances local business elites are usually content to work, as they do in Norwalk, with an outdated set of land-use laws. The efficacy of policies which build on local trends in land-use conversion can be illustrated through a discussion of policies to provide low-income suburban housing and assert local control over developers.

Low-income housing in the suburbs

With the deconcentration of the American population over the past 30 years the residential divisions between upper and lower-classes have begun to coincide with municipal boundaries (Ostrom, 1983; Schneider and Logan, 1982). Under these conditions affluent communities have used their taxing power to create further advantages for their residents in the quest for property, credentials, and the amenities of life. To reduce these new forms of inequality, political activists of a liberal persuasion have advocated "opening up the suburbs" so as to permit the construction of low-income housing in these communities (Downs, 1973). In the mid 1970s Michael Danielson (1976:327) concluded a review of opening housing advocacy on a pessimistic note.

Considering the widespread opposition, lack of support from most of the excluded, and meager results from past efforts, one can reasonably ask whether opening the suburbs is worth the trouble.

Renewed questioning about the efficacy of this policy occurred in the late 1970s when a small number of built-up, affluent suburbs, under heavy political pressure, altered their zoning laws so as to permit multi-family housing. The legal change did not produce much social change. After Westport amended its zoning ordinance to permit apartments for the first time, one observer remarked,

In adopting tight restrictions on the height, number, and density of the apartments that will be allowed, Westport adhered to the same principle that governs single family zoning in many suburban towns: big lots, few people.[2]

Even when the zoning regulations do not require expensive housing, the presence of an expensive, well-maintained housing stock on adjacent tracts of land makes it difficult to build subsidized, low-income housing on these sites. Under the provisions of the Housing and Urban Development Act of

1968 a developer has to devote only 10 percent of the units in a development to low-income housing in order to qualify for federal subsidies. With an eye to his profit margin the developer makes the remaining 90 percent of the units large and spacious. Not surprisingly these units carry a hefty price tag. In size, design, and price they resemble the single-family homes on adjacent tracts of land. In this case a change in land-use control had little effect on the supply of low-income housing. If effective controls almost always reflect an ongoing process of conversion, it should not be surprising that imposed controls encounter considerable opposition and, when enacted, produce results which the reformers neither desired nor expected. Following the logic of the conversion-control link outlined earlier, effective strategies of providing low-income housing in suburban settings would be founded on visible trends in local housing markets. Two trends in the 1970s come to mind; one involves developers who began to construct attached housing in rural–urban fringe communities; the other involves homeowners who began to create accessory apartments in urban communities.

Proposals to provide low-income housing which take advantage of market forces stand a greater chance of approval than proposals which ignore these trends. A comparison of attitudes towards apartment complexes in rural–urban fringe communities and inner suburbs provides a case in point. Because land uses in suburbs are more homogeneous than land uses in fringe communities, landowners in the suburbs show more uniformity in their opinions about land-use changes than do landowners in fringe areas. Popular responses to proposals for multi-family housing follow this pattern. In suburbs the homeowners, who comprise 95 percent of the landowners, oppose the construction of multi-family housing projects. In fringe areas attitudes toward multi-family housing are mixed. Homeowners object, but the owners of undeveloped land often support efforts to build multi-family housing because these projects increase the demand for undeveloped land. These political circumstances suggest that attached housing should be easier to construct in fringe areas.

The geography of new multi-family housing during the 1960s and 1970s confirms this impression. Attached housing projects in rural–urban fringe communities exceeded those in suburbs in number as well as in scale. Consistent with the generally more permissive regulatory policies pursued in peripheral communities, zoning commissioners in fringe communities such as Brookfield or Southbury allowed the first two or three developers who proposed multi-family complexes to build them. Compared with the immense difficulties of constructing multi-family housing in inner suburbs, the short-lived successes in the construction of multi-family housing in fringe communities suggest that peripheral communities offer the only politically feasible locations outside of cities for low income, multi-family housing.

The disappointing results of attempts to build low-income housing in the inner suburbs leave unanswered the question of how best to "open up" these communities. Rather than trying to force suburban populations to accept multi-unit housing, advocates should take note of the declining household sizes and growing numbers of in-house apartments in suburbs. Because these apartments rent for modest sums of money and because they tend to occur in the large homes which predominate in affluent areas, the creation of accessory apartments should contribute to the economic desegregation of the wealthiest neighborhoods in the metropolitan area. Activists could promote this trend by arguing for the abolition of laws prohibiting in-house apartments in affluent suburbs.

Because the owners of in-house apartments exercise more discretion and probably discriminate more in the choice of tenants than the owners of multi-unit structures, in-house apartments will not house the same type of low-income population as apartment complexes. Studies in middle-income Long Island suburbs indicate that the apartments contain disproportionate numbers of low-income white persons (Rudel, 1984b). In this sense accessory apartments promise to further the economic but not the racial desegregation of the suburbs. In effect by legalizing in-house apartments, policymakers would expedite the "trickle down" process which has traditionally provided housing for poor households. Given the resounding lack of success which open-housing advocates have had in promoting the construction of multi-family housing in suburbs, they would do well to push for the legalization of in-house apartments.

These considerations suggest that low-income housing policies should be situation specific. In pursuing the goal of open housing in fringe areas where the construction of new units is common, policymakers should promote the construction of low-income units; in pursuing the same goal in urban communities where the conversion of units is widespread, policymakers should promote the conversion of units into in-house apartments. Because these housing policies build on processes already under way in the market, they stand a greater chance of enactment and are more likely to produce significant amounts of low-income housing than policies which are blind to local variations in processes of real estate development.

Developers' reputations and local residents' expectations as instruments in land-use policymaking

In Keith Hawkins' probing study of water pollution control a government enforcement officer remarked that "you generally know where to look for trouble" (1984:93). In other words variations in potential polluters' past performances make it possible for the enforcement officers to identify those firms which are most likely to pollute. Using the same sources of knowledge, local land-use authorities can identify those developers whose projects are most likely to cause significant environmental problems. Land-use laws are not, however, written so as to encourage the use of this information in regulating developers. Two examples of this information and how it might be used in a reformed set of laws are presented below. One example comes from an urban setting; the other example comes from a rural setting.

Because most developers in urban areas build repeatedly in the same local area, they acquire reputations among planners. The reputations have an evaluative dimension; some developers become notorious because they try to cut corners in virtually every project which they build; the SKG corporation in New Milford exemplifies this type of builder; other developers consistently do high-quality work. By law local land-use authorities must treat both developers the same way, creating what Scholz (1984) calls an enforcement dilemma. Under lax regulation the notorious developer can cut corners; under restrictive regulation the reputable developer suffers unnecessary regulation. These problems can be resolved if communities adopt procedures which are sensitive to a developer's performance on previous projects. If a developer incurs the wrath of purchasers in one project by cutting corners, the planners could penalize him on his next project by subjecting it to extraordinary scrutiny. Similarly developers whose previous projects did not generate controversy over shoddy construction could be rewarded with more cursory regulation on their next project. In effect planners would be applying a 'tit-for-tat' strategy in dealing with developers. Axelrod's research (1984) suggests that over time this type of policy would produce cooperative behavior, in this case quality construction, among developers.

The experience of local governments in rural areas with conventional land-use policy suggests that a modified form of the tit for tat policy might be effective in rural areas. Local governments in rural areas usually do not exercise legal controls over land use (Rudel, 1984a). The absence of controls only becomes an issue when an outside developer proposes to build in a community. A land-use planner for the state of Utah recalls numerous requests for emergency assistance from local officials. The problem was simple. In one official's words, "We need to pass some zoning because some guy has put an application in here."[3]

If rural populations often do not have the regulations which they would like, they just as frequently find themselves saddled with regulations which they do not want. Two examples from western Connecticut illustrate this connection. The town of Southbury adopted land-use controls in 1940 in order to prevent the German Bund, a group of Nazi sympathizers, from establishing a summer camp in town. In Goshen adoption occurred in the late 1950s when exurbanites pushed through a law at a poorly attended town meeting. In both Goshen and Southbury, landowners who had few plans for developing their land suddenly found themselves subject to regulations which restricted the use of land. Not surprisingly, the imposition of controls, in circumstances which did not indicate a need for them, aroused the opposition which later led to the repeal of the laws.

In sum, rural communities seem to have either too many or too few controls over land use. In places with legal controls the commissioners subject small developments to unnecessary regulation while they await the infrequent proposals for large-scale developments. In places without controls small developers do not suffer from unnecessary regulation, but the community has no means of controlling the occasional large-scale development. In both types of places regulatory problems occur because the controls do not reflect the conversion process. "Complaint zoning" founded on the informal means of social control so prevalent in rural communities, offers a potential solution to this problem. Under this system enforcement is on a complaint basis. The community has a set of land-use regulations, but they only apply to proposals which elicit complaints from community residents. If no one complains about a proposed development within a designated period of time, the developer may proceed to build. If a resident registers an objection, the developer must have his project reviewed by the zoning commission.

Citizen complaints under this system follow a pattern. No one complains about the minor problems created by the small-scale projects of local developers, but plans by outside developers for large-scale developments invariably generate complaints. Neighboring landowners may also complain when a developer with a questionable reputation proposes to build near them. The system is not perfect. One must assume that locally based, large-scale developers would be exempt from control under this system. While examples of formalized complaint zoning are rare, it has several features which recommend it for use in rural locales (Barrows and Olson, 1981). Like performance zoning, it recognizes differences in the effects of different-sized projects on adjacent landowners and exempts most small projects from regulation. Unlike performance zoning, which requires the services of experts to measure spillover effects, complaint zoning relies on local residents' expectations about spillover effects, so it will not be as precise in its estimates as performance zoning, but it will be within the financial means of small town governments.

Because a developer's reputation will frequently affect whether or not local residents complain about a proposed development, complaint zoning resembles the tit-for-tat planning strategy outlined above. Both policies use information from previous development projects to guide responses to proposals for new developments. In the importance which they attribute to developers' reputations and residents' expectations about development, the reforms acknowledge that development is an iterative process in which the developers and planners come together numerous times over a period of years. Following game theoretic notions, the reforms attempt to use the iterative nature of this process to induce cooperative behavior among developers.

Conclusion

The discussions of low-income housing and developer reputations argue for the effectiveness of policies which build on local variations in land markets and use local residents' knowledge of developers. Applied to highly touted innovations in land-use planning such as performance zoning and the transfer of development rights, these lessons imply that we will not reap the full benefits of these reforms until we have identified the processes for which they are the appropriate controls. Without a detailed understanding of the political and economic processes which would make these innovations attractive to landowners, planners will apply them in inappropriate situations, and the reforms will meet with popular rejection.

While a clairvoyant elite may on occasion acknowledge the importance of local trends and local concerns in land-use planning, this orientation is more likely to develop in circumstances in which most land users have some influence over land-use authorities. Ordinary land users are often the first to experience a change in land-use conversion. If these land users have some influence with land-use authorities, legal changes which provide some relief from the negative effects of land-use changes are more likely to be forthcoming. In sum, more effective land-use planning may require a concerted effect to democratize the regulation of real estate development. In substance this program of reform will vary by community. In suburbs it may involve measures to insure the presence of disadvantaged, elderly home-owners in decision making processes; in cities it may involve legislation to facilitate citizen initiatives in land-use planning. In both instances the reforms would increase the likelihood that land-use authorities will pursue policies which reflect the sentiments of a wide range of their constituents. At the very least this type of institutional order should produce more efficacious, intelligent tinkering with land-use laws in thousands of American communities.

Appendix A Changes in land-use controls: multivariate analyses

The adoption of land-use laws

In most Connecticut communities a single proposal to develop land prompted the adoption of land-use controls. In 1936 a farmer subdivided his land along Lake Waramaug into 13 separate lots and broke ground on the first 'development' in Warren. The traffic to and from the new homes disturbed the "peace and quiet" of a prominent summer resident to the point where he felt justified in going to the board of selectmen with his problems. After hearing his complaints about the noise and dust from passing cars, the board enacted the community's first land-use law. In 1972 in Kent a businessman, who had built several single-stall car washes, drew up plans for a five-stall car wash. When a homeowner living near the site first heard of the plan, she had visions of cars pulling up to the car wash day and night. Convinced that the proposed development was not in keeping with the "tranquil, small town" character of Kent, the apprehensive resident contacted her neighbors, and together they circulated a petition calling for the adoption of land-use controls. In a referendum several weeks later, the community adopted a zoning law. In 1973 a Hartford radio station decided to build a large transmitting station in Morris. The station consisted of a small building and a 200-foot tower. Several nearby landowners objected to the project because the tower would obstruct the view east from their homes and increase traffic on the road in front of their homes. To prevent the construction of the tower, they circulated a petition calling for the adoption of a land-use law which would prohibit the construction of radio towers in the town. Several weeks later the voters in Morris approved the adoption of land-use controls by a narrow margin. In 1970 in Litchfield a developer's plan to build a 300-unit subdivision prompted a political movement which culminated in the adoption of legal controls over land use. In 1972 in Sharon rumors that a developer was buying up land north of the town spurred the adoption of a land-use law. The 13-lot subdivision in Warren, the five-stall car wash in Kent, the radio tower in Morris, and the residential developments in Litchfield and Sharon all represented dramatic changes in the scale or type of real estate development in these towns, and in each case news of the proposed development triggered a political campaign which resulted in the adoption of a zoning law.

The prospect of large-scale real estate development does not always result in the adoption of land-use controls. For example, in Goshen in the early 1970s the voters rejected land-use controls several months after a group of farmers made public their plans to build a large recreational real estate development around Woodbridge Lake. Variations across communities in the political strength of exurbanite and farming factions along with differences in the timing of changes in the type of development should predict when a community will adopt a land-use law. An analysis of the year in which each of the 31 communities in western Connecticut adopted a zoning law provides a test for this hypothesis. The measure for the development variable is indirect. Because real estate developments change in type and scale when a community is incorporated into a metropolitan area, communities closer to the metropolitan center should experience changes in real estate development well before communities located farther from the metropolitan center. For this reason the distance of a community from the metropolitan center, in this case New York City, provides a measure of the change in land-use conversion which presumably triggers the passage of land-use laws. A topographical variable provides a predictor of the balance of power between exurbanites and farmers. This measure, drawn from the 1929 agricultural census, is the percentage of all land in the town in farms. If a town had little land in farms in 1929, it probably has rugged topography, numerous scenic sites for second homes, and in the post World War II period a large fraction of exurbanites in local politics. By taking the data from a census prior to the onset of suburbanization in the region, the percentage of land in farms reflects topographical differences between communities rather than differences in the degree to which communities have become built up.

The results of the regression analysis, reported in table 10, support the hypothesis outlined above. The juxtaposition of data on the first five and last five communities to adopt land-use controls indicates the general pattern of adoption. The ability of the equation to explain a considerable amount (37 percent) of the variance suggests that the configuration of interests which resulted in the passage of land-use laws in the mid 1940s may not have differed dramatically from the configuration of interests which resulted in the passage of land-use controls in the mid 1970s. The significance of the partial regression coefficients indicates that differences in the timing of changes in real estate development and, to a lesser extent, differences in topography explain

Table 10. *The adoption of land-use laws*

Panel A: The pattern of adoption in ten communities

Date of adoption	Distance from New York city	% of town land in farms, 1929
1929	65	45
1932	80	59
1936	85	40
1938	85	52
1938	99	46
1972	108	47
1975	90	70
1980[a]	85	85
1980[a]	98	63
1980[a]	100	62

Panel B: Regression analysis of the pattern of adoption in 31 Communities

Date zoned $= 1902 + 0.526$ Distance from New York** +
$\qquad$ (0.156)
$\qquad$ 0.276 Farmland, 1929*
$\qquad$ (0.141)
$\qquad r = 0.607, r^2 = 0.369, n = 31, p < 0.01$

** < 0.05, * < 0.10

[a] Because three communities had not adopted zoning laws by the date when this data was collected, the sample is right censored on three cases. While censoring problems can cause bias, the small number of censored cases (3 out of 31) in this analysis suggests that the biases introduced by censoring are small and would not alter the general conclusions drawn from this analysis.

Source: Archives of 31 Connecticut municipalities; Connecticut Department of Transportation; Agricultural Census, Connecticut, 1929.

why some communities adopted land-use controls as early as the 1930s while other communities waited until the 1970s to institute controls.

Increases in the restrictiveness of controls

One might expect significant increases in the restrictiveness of zoning laws only in those peripheral communities which have had large numbers of farms within their borders because only these communities combined the uncertainties of rapid rates of development with the permissive land-use laws whose reform could be expected to change the direction of development

Table 11. *The pattern of increasing restriction in land-use control: a regression analysis*

Zoning Change = 3.20 + 0.950 Change in Farmers/Labor Force*
(0.420)
* = $p < .05$

Sources: Zoning Ordinances, Twenty Connecticut Municipalities; Town and County Fact Books, 1960, 1970.

in a community. Presumably a rapid rate of development, by causing a rapid decline in the number of farmers and a rapid increase in the number of homeowners, would diminish the opposition to restrictive land-use controls at the same time that it generated demands for more restrictive regulations. Data on changes in western Connecticut land-use laws between 1960 and 1970 make it possible to test this hypothesis.

The decline in the proportion of farmers in a community's labor force between 1960 and 1970 provided an indirect measure of both the size of the original farming community and the speed of land-use conversion in the community. A large decline between 1960 and 1970 would suggest both a relatively large farming community at the beginning of suburbanization and a rapid rate of land-use conversion during the 1960–1970 decade. The measure of restrictiveness in land-use controls proved difficult to construct. Homeowners, builders, and town officials have a common, casually held understanding of what constitutes a 'restrictive' or 'permissive' zoning law. When pressed to define what they mean by a restrictive or permissive law, most people cite the number of permitted land uses or the minimum lot area required for building houses. Generally land-use laws are restrictive if they limit development to tracts of land above a minimum size and permit only one or two uses of these lands. Using a zoning map and ordinance, these popular understandings of a permissive or a restrictive law can be converted into a single interval level measure of the degree of restriction. The resulting measure indicates the average number of land uses permitted per acre in the town. Permissive ordinances allow many uses and restrictive ordinances allow few uses, so a decline over time in the number of permitted uses means that a law has become more restrictive.

Because only 20 of the 31 communities had zoning ordinances in both 1960 and 1970, the analysis was limited to 20 communities. The results are presented in table 11. They indicate that increases in the degree of restriction occurred in those communities which experienced large declines in the numbers of farmers during the 1960s. By implication land-use laws probably became more restrictive when, in the face of rapid real estate development, middle-class homeowners in farmer dominated communities pressured for up-zonings as a means of assuring the middle-class or, if possible, upper-class status of the neighborhoods in which they lived.

Appendix B Survey methods

Interviews with landowners in four widely separated places provided the data for the ethnographic accounts of real estate development reported in chapters 4, 5, and 6. A brief account of the sampling strategies and interviewing procedures used to collect these data is presented below.

The universe

The four neighborhoods were chosen on the basis of two criteria. First, the pattern of land use in each neighborhood appeared to be 'typical' of its community. Secondly, each neighborhood was undergoing some form of real estate development at the time of the study. The decision to study neighborhoods undergoing development rested on practical considerations in data collection. The choice of developing neighborhoods increased the probability that landowners would have an active interest in the issues surrounding real estate development and would be well informed about the history of real estate development in their neighborhood.

These two criteria for choosing neighborhoods conflicted with one another in the slow-growing, core communities. Representative neighborhoods in these communities usually were not experiencing any real estate development, so choosing neighborhoods under development introduced a bias into the accounts of real estate development in the core communities. Because the residents of developing neighborhoods attribute greater importance to issues of land-use control than do the residents of already developed neighborhoods, the bias in the sample of neighborhoods would make it easy to exaggerate the degree of popular concern with issues of land-use control. Because the analysis of core community land-use planning does not rest on assertions about the overall level of interest in land-use planning, this source of error would not appear to affect the analysis in crucial ways.

The respondents were selected through multi-stage area sampling techniques (Warwick and Lininger, 1975: 111–125). The size of the sampled areas varied with the population density of places. In the rural and rural–urban fringe areas where the densities were lower, the sampled areas were larger. In Goshen the universe included all residents living within one mile of a second home development; in New Milford the universe included all those residents living within one-half mile of the proposed site for a subdivision of single-family homes. In the urban communities the radius of the sampled area was one-quarter mile. The rationale for the differences in the size of the sampled areas involved a judgment that the proposed developments would have more far-reaching effects in rural than in urban locales. In rural locales where everyone in the community uses the same roads, schools, and stores, the increased congestion caused by an influx of new residents would affect every resident in the community. In urban areas with their much larger numbers of roads, schools, and stores, the increase in congestion would not extend beyond the catchment areas for these local facilities. The sampling fractions in the peripheral communities were larger than they were in the core communities. In the peripheral communities about one out of every five households was chosen for an interview; in the core communities the sampling fraction was one out of every ten households.

Street directories provided the list of households from which the respondents were drawn. Because developers are reluctant to build in lower-class neighborhoods, the study was limited to lower-middle, middle, and upper-class neighborhoods. Over 90 percent of the households in these neighborhoods have telephones. Given the high proportion of households with telephones, the use of a street directory to draw the sample probably did not result in significant selection biases. Once a household had been selected, I requested an interview with an adult member of the household. I made the initial contact call in the early evening so as to insure that working men and women as well as housewives and retired persons would be represented in the sample.

The choice of this sampling strategy involved several considerations. I decided to gather the oral histories by means of a randomly selected sample of local residents rather than through a snowball sample of people who, by reputation, knew a great deal about local real estate development. While longtime residents would, without a doubt, have had the most information about the history of real estate development in a particular neighborhood, it is also clear that, especially in rural and rural–urban fringe locales, longtime residents had a set of interests in land which differed in important ways from the interests of newcomers in the neighborhood. Because the survey was designed not only to build an historical account of local real estate development, but also to explore the interrelationship between the present composition of landed interests in a neighborhood and the reactions of landowners to proposed developments, a snowball sample would not have yielded a representative sample of residents. By choosing to select a random sample, I sacrificed depth in the historical accounts for representativeness in the sample.

Interviewing procedures

Having drawn a sample of households, I wrote a letter to the head of each household introducing the study and requesting an interview with an adult member of the household. Several days after the selected households had received the letter, I called to arrange an interview. If I could not reach a household by phone, I would stop by and arrange in person the time and place of the interview.

Questions

The survey instrument was a semi-structured questionnaire with separate sections on local real estate development, the effects of development on daily living, personal data, and the respondent's residential history.

Questions 1–6 focused on current and past real estate development in the neighborhood. Question 1 asked the respondent for his opinion about the current proposal for development in the neighborhood. Questions 2 through 6 concerned the history of real estate development in the neighborhood. Question 2 asked the respondent to list the major land-use changes which had taken place during his residence in the neighborhood. Questions 3 through 6 focused on particular land-use changes. For each land-use change the respondents were asked how they first found out about the proposed development, what their initial reaction to the proposed land use was, and what, if any, type of political action they took. These questions were asked in an open-ended way, and the respondents were encouraged to expand on their accounts of what happened when the development was first proposed. Because all of the landowners lived in the same area, there was a large amount of overlap in the events about which they spoke. As a result during the course of interviewing in a neighborhood I would get as many as 10 to 15 accounts of the circumstances surrounding the development of a particular piece of land. This overlap provided me with numerous occasions for verifying and cross-checking the assertions and details of earlier accounts of a land-use conversion. Through this process of winnowing and sifting, a general account of the circumstances surrounding a particular real estate development would emerge. These accounts formed the basis for much of the ethnographic material presented in chapters 4 through 6.

The second section of the questionnaire concerned the effects of nearby real estate developments on the daily routines of the respondents. Questions 7 through 15 asked about the individual's personal experience with problems associated with urbanization in the community. Specific questions concerned experiences with crime, traffic congestion, parking problems, automobile accidents, congestion in stores and at recreational facilities, and a hypothetical question designed to measure the respondent's sensitivity to problems of congestion. This section ended with several questions about the extent of local air and water pollution.

Questions 16 through 27 concerned the personal characteristics of the respondent. Questions about the frequency of neighborhood interactions and the flexibility of daily routines provided information which made it possible to entertain hypotheses about variations in the effects of these projects on individuals. Other questions concerned important personal characteristics such as age, sex, occupation, education, income, and place of work. To this information I added information from the town tax records about the respondent's holdings of land and other taxable property.

Questions 28 through 35 concerned the respondent's residential history. Answers to these questions provided information on the individual's last four places of residence, his childhood home, and his current place of residence. Several other questions asked about the respondent's expectations, plans, or desires for future residential mobility. The final question returned to the central theme of the interview by asking for the respondent's opinion about future real estate development in his neighborhood.

The response rate and possible biases

Table 12 provides data on the response rates for each of the four communities in which the case studies were carried out. Because most of the interviewing was carried out during the summer months, an unusual number of respondents could not be reached, presumably because they were away on vacations. Of those heads of households contacted, more than 82 percent agreed to be interviewed. Those people who refused to be interviewed usually did so because they were "too busy" or "not interested" in real estate development in their neighborhood. All of the interviews which were begun were completed. Women predominated among the refusals, perhaps because the request for an interview came from an unknown male. Of the women

Table 12. *Response rates by community*

Field procedures: numbers of respondents

Community	Called	Contacted	Interviewed	Refused interview	Response rate
Goshen	42	37	30	7	0.811
New Milford	41	37	30	7	0.811
Norwalk	39	34	30	4	0.866
Westport	43	39	31	8	0.795
Totals	165	147	121	26	0.823

Source: sampling frames in possession of the author.

contacted, 22.4 percent refused to be interviewed; of the males contacted, 12.8 percent refused to be interviewed. If the information from the interviews was being analyzed statistically, this bias in the sample might have resulted in a corresponding bias in the analysis, but because, the interview data are being used largely to create plausible accounts of how real estate development occurred in a neighborhood and because the sample already contains large numbers of women, the female perspective on nearby land-use changes appears to have been represented in a way which would not seriously bias the analysis.

Notes

1 Introduction: local governments and land-use planning

1 The value of the non-residential construction is in 1980 dollars. Sources: US Department of Commerce, Bureau of the Census, Housing Construction Statistics, 1889–1964, table A-1, p. 18; U.S. Department of Commerce, Bureau of the Census, Housing Starts, March, 1982, table 1, p. 3; US Department of Commerce, Bureau of the Census, Value of New Construction Put in Place in the United States, 1964–1980, tables 1, D-1, pp. 4, 183.

2 Telephone Interview, Donna Corley, Planner, Tennessee Valley Regional Council of Governments, June 25, 1983.

3 Steve Ellwanger, "Bound Brook battle continues; lawsuits open in court May 2." The Norwalk *Hour*, April 26, 1979.

4 In planning parlance the intensity of a land use refers to the extent of human investment in the land. The investment can be in either monetary or human terms. Generally the more built-up a tract of land and the more people who use its facilities during a particular period of time, the more intense the land use will be.

5 Case studies of local land-use control are numerous. The following list includes only the most prominent of these studies. For center cities, see Walter Firey, *Land Use in Central Boston* (1947); Sidney Willhelm, *Urban Zoning and Land Use Theory* (1962); and Francine Rabinowitz, *City Planning and Politics* (1969). For suburbs, see Mary Anne Guitar, *Property Power* (1972); Robert A. Lemire, *Creative Land Development: Bridge to the Future* (1979); Samuel Kaplan, *The Dream Deferred: People, Politics, and Planning in Suburbia* (1976); and David Dowall, *The Suburban Squeeze: Land Conversion and Regulation in the San Francisco Bay Area* (1984). For rural–urban fringe areas, see Alvin Socolow, *Government Response to Urbanization: Three Townships on the Rural–urban Fringe* (1968); and Mark Gottdiener, *Planned Sprawl: Public and Private Interests in Suburbia* (1977). For rural areas, see Ann Louise Strong, *Private Property and the Public Interest* (1975); Jane J. Mansbridge, *Beyond Adversary Democracy* (1980); and Boyd Gibbons, *Wye Island: Outsiders and Resistance to Change* (1977).

2 Situations and strategies in local land-use control

1 Pierre Clavel's recent work (1986) is an exception to this generalization.

2 Typically, growth coalitions will involve individuals drawn from a variety of occupations: builders, realtors, bankers; lawyers, and local public officials. In the proceedings which surround land-use planning some members of growth coalitions are more prominent than others, notably the builders who must present and defend proposals for development. On the other hand bankers, while extremely important to the operation of growth coalitions, have little to do with land-use planning and appear infrequently in the case studies described in the following chapters.

3 One must be careful about definitions of mobility. For residents who have resided in an area for a long time but plan to move when they retire, the shadow of the future may not loom large, and they may not be cooperative in planning their land uses.

4 Michael Winerip, "One man's efforts conserve Catskills valley," The New York *Times*, February 19, 1985.

5 For Williamson (1975:9) "opportunism refers to a lack of candor or honesty in transactions, to include self-interest seeking with guile."

6 The low level of political activity surrounding these proposals may have changed somewhat in the 1970s and 1980s with the increased sensitivity of farmers on the rural–urban fringe to the problems for farm operations caused by nearby subdivisions of single-family homes (Thompson, 1980). These conflicts have led to the passage of "right to farm" laws in more than 20 states.

3 Suburban development and land-use planning in western Connecticut

1 The terms 'core' and 'periphery' refer to the location of the community in the metropolitan area. Core communities have an older housing stock and less undeveloped land than peripheral communities do.

2 In deciding on a site for the field research, I seriously considered the Tampa – St. Petersburg metropolitan area before settling on a metropolitan area in the northeastern United States.

3 One could object to the choice of this region on the grounds that none of the communities in western Connecticut are rural. A comparative analysis of the degree of rurality in 67 New England counties responds to this criticism (Babin and Field, 1977). The analysis included Litchfield County in northwestern Connecticut which contains the rural communities in this study. Creating indices of rurality out of 1970 census data, the authors established an overall measure of how rural a county was. Using this measure, Litchfield County appeared to be as rural as counties in western Massachusetts, central Vermont, and central New Hampshire. More generally, the rural communities in the sample appear to be representative of the 'interstitial' rural areas of the metropolitan belt which extends from southern Maine to northern Virginia (Beale, 1981: 54–55).

4 These are average figures for 19 contiguous towns in northwestern Connecticut. Sources: 1929 and 1974 Agricultural Censuses.

5 These figures were computed from municipal property tax records, all of which distinguish between developed and undeveloped land.

6 The data on patterns of landholdings and on changes in patterns of landholding were gathered by drawing random samples of landholdings from the tax records of each of the 31 municipalities for 1960 and again for 1970. A weighted combination of the municipal samples produced the regional sample for both 1960 and 1970. From these samples the regional pattern of landholdings for each year was calculated.

7 Because agricultural and residential landowners comprise more than 95 percent of all land users in western Connecticut, the shifts depicted in figure 3 are predominantly shifts in the distribution of land among these owners.

8 The inclusion of two towns, both located along Route 7, in the I-84 corridor requires some comment. Although they are not particularly close to I-84, I included them in the I-84 corridor because their location on Route 7, a heavily traveled road which intersects I-84, makes traveling time between the two towns and I-84 much less than it is for other towns which, although a similar distance from I-84, have no thoroughfare connecting them with the turnpike.

9 The 50 percent decline in the price of land in the I-84 corridor requires some explanation. It occurred because the construction of the new road through a rural–urban fringe area into a hitherto inaccessible rural area expands the size of the fringe area considerably. The sudden growth in the size of the fringe area increases the supply of undeveloped land available for development, and this increase in supply causes the decline in price. When a large amount of land is rezoned to permit commercial and industrial uses in a community, a similar effect on the prices of other parcels of commercial or industrial land can be observed; the prices of these parcels decline in the period immediately after the rezoning (Lorimer, 1972:164).

10 Appendix A presents a regression analysis of variations in the dates when communities adopted their first land-use controls. A topographical variable and distance from New York City proved to be the best predictors.

11 Minutes, New Milford Planning and Zoning Commission, 1970.

12 Editorial, "Town meeting." The New Milford *Times*, January 8, 1970.

13 Rene Wendelken, "Letter to the editor." The Litchfield *Enquirer*, March 25, 1976.

14 Sources: Town and County Fact Book, 1970; Housing Characteristics for Towns and Counties, 1970.

15 Art Cummings, "New first selectman: a symbol of New Milford's rural past." The New Milford *Times*, July 14, 1977.

16 Names and place names have been changed in the neighborhood studies in order to prevent the identification of respondents.

4 A rural community

1 The terms "relational controls" and "informal controls" are used interchangeably throughout this chapter. "Legal or rule-based controls" are synonymous with "formal controls."

2 Anonymous interviews, Goshen and Morris homeowners, August, 1977.

3 Flyer, Citizen's Committee for an Unzoned Norfolk, Norfolk, Connecticut, 1972.
4 Anonymous interview, Morris homeowner, June, 1975.
5 Data source: minutes, Goshen Planning Commission, 1979.
6 Anonymous interviews, Goshen homeowners, June, July, 1977.
7 Vandalized property usually provides the impetus behind decisions to post land, and because their property is vandalized more often, absentee landowners tend to post their land more frequently than resident owners do. See New Hampshire Fish and Game Department (1971).
8 Anonymous interview, Goshen homeowner, July, 1977.
9 Anonymous interviews, Goshen homeowners, July, 1977.
10 Samuel G. Freedman, "Tiny Connecticut town in a big housing battle." The New York *Times*, May 17, 1982.
11 Ibid.
12 For an interesting examination of this attitude toward the land, see Fred Bosselman, "The world as a park," in Richard L. Andrews (1979).
13 Transcript by a court reporter at an official town meeting called to consider the repeal of zoning, Goshen, Connecticut, October 16, 1967. On file in the Goshen Town Hall.
14 Anonymous interview, Goshen resident, July, 1977.
15 Data source: minutes, Goshen Planning Commission, 1979.
16 Anonymous interviews, Goshen homeowners, July, August, 1977.
17 Transcript, Goshen Town Meeting, p. 8.
18 Katherine Walker, quoted in the Waterbury *Republican*, September 17, 1974.
19 Dr Phillip C. Jessup, quoted in Childs, 1975, p. 11.
20 Thomas Goodenough, quoted in Childs, 1975, p. 14.
21 Transcript, Goshen Town Meeting, p. 16.
22 Anonymous interview, Morris homeowner, May, 1978.
23 Interview, Chairman of the Planning and Zoning Commission, Kent, Connecticut, August, 1978.
24 Minutes, Morris Planning and Zoning Commission, August, 1962.
25 Interview, Planning and Zoning Commissioner, Roxbury, August, 1978.
26 Anonymous interview, Planning Commissioner, Goshen, August 1977.
27 Anonymous interview, Goshen homeowner, June, 1977.
28 Response to a survey of citizen attitudes toward zoning conducted by the town government's Zoning Study Committee, Morris, 1973. On file in the Morris Town Hall.
29 "Planning and Zoning Commission resignation in Morris," The Litchfield *Enquirer*, December 7, 1963.
30 Anonymous interview, Planning Commissioner, Goshen, July, 1977.
31 Ibid.
32 Anonymous interview, Realtor, Kent, April, 1975.
33 Interview, Secretary, Planning and Zoning Commission, Cornwall, January, 1975.
34 "Arrow Point controversy continues." The New Milford *Times*, March 7, 1968.

35 For an explanation of the general conditions under which false unanimity arises, see Mansbridge (1980:276–277).

5 A rural–urban fringe community

1 White Plains and Paramus are suburban cities in the New York metropolitan area. White Plains has a small, but well-known low-income area while Paramus has one of the largest concentrations of shopping centers in the eastern United States.
2 Peter H. Helmer, "Southbury halts business growth." The Danbury *News-Times*, April 6, 1975.
3 Announcements: Coalition to Stop Route 7.
4 Anonymous interview, New Milford homeowner, June, 1977.
5 Editorial, "As we see it: from the sublime." The New Milford *Times*, July 3, 1968.
6 Anonymous interviews, New Milford homeowners, July, August, 1978.
7 Elaine Hall, "You buy a $95,000 home, and you can't drink the water." The New Milford *Times*, October 2, 1980; Erni Hamlin, "Too many omissions charged to developer." The New Milford *Times*, February 2, 1980; editorial, "SKG's string of mistakes." The New Milford *Times*, February 14, 1980; Jim Stuart, "A reporter's notebook." The New Milford *Times*, February 14, 1980.
8 Bob Barraclough, "A story of frustration: it's always someone else's problem." The New Milford *Times*, June 3, 1968.
9 Ibid.
10 Anonymous interview, Fox Hill homeowner, New Milford, July, 1978.
11 Anonymous interview, Fox Hill homeowner, New Milford, July, 1978.
12 Anonymous interviews, Fox Hill homeowners, New Milford, August, 1978.
13 Anonymous interview, Fox Hill homeowner, New Milford, June, 1978.
14 Anonymous interviews, Fox Hill homeowners, New Milford, July, 1978.
15 Anonymous interview, Town Planner, Wilton, February, 1975.
16 Anonymous interview, former member of the New Milford planning and zoning commission, August, 1978.
17 The most consistent pressure for increases in the restrictions over land use came from residents of upper-income areas in middle-income communities. For an analysis of changes in the restrictiveness of regulations across 20 western Connecticut communities, see section two of appendix B.
18 Erni Hamlin, "Planning chair to Oskar Rogg." The New Milford *Times*, October 18, 1979.
19 Editorial, "SKG's string of mistakes."
20 Elaine Hall, "Crescent Lane residents disgruntled with officials." The New Milford *Times*, October 16, 1980.
21 Elaine Hall, "You buy a $95,000 home…"
22 Editorial, "Promises can be broken." The New Milford *Times*, March 3, 1981.
23 Peter Kosta, "Conflict of interest regulations voted down." The New Milford *Times*, October 1, 1981.
24 Editorial, "The public is a no-show." The New Milford *Times*, August 9, 1979; editorial, "Courage of her convictions." The New Milford *Times*, October 11,

1979; Erni Hamlin, "Partners survey their tough business." The New Milford *Times*, November 1, 1979.

25 Data source: minutes, New Milford Planning and Zoning Commission; interview with New Milford zoning inspector.

26 Anonymous interview, New Milford newspaper reporter, August, 1978.

27 Anonymous interview, Fox Hill homeowner, New Milford, July, 1978.

28 Anonymous interviews, Fox Hill homeowners, New Milford, June, July, 1978.

29 Anonymous interview, New Milford newspaper reporter, July, 1978; editorial, "We're confused." The New Milford *Times*, December 24, 1969.

30 The implication here that large developers build more defects into homes than do small developers should be qualified. It may well be that the largest developers, who often provide a warranty with their houses, build a more structurally sound house than the houses built by the middle-sized 'starter' home developers in New Milford. See Eichler (1982:102, 229).

31 Erni Hamlin, "Colonial Ridge intervenors: they're disappointed in the planning panel." The New Milford *Times*, November 8, 1979.

32 Circular, "Neighbors for New Milford," Summer, 1978.

6 Urban communities

1 Robert Correia, "Population down, housing up." The Norwalk *Hour*, July 29, 1980.

2 "Only 38% of Westporters approve town planning." The Westport *Town Crier*, October 29, 1953.

3 Editorial, "Westport: ideal living place or topsy town?" The Westport *Town Crier*, April 23, 1953.

4 Editorial, "What's happening to Westport." The Westport *Town Crier*, December 16, 1954.

5 Quoted in Jeff Silverstein, "Lower cost homes will be forced by courts, town told." The Westport *News*, October 27, 1976.

6 The building statistics came from the Annual Reports of the Town of Westport, 1960 and 1980.

7 "Silvermine wins its fight to shut out business; Zoning Board heeds pleas to keep it residential." The Norwalk *Hour*, March 22, 1940.

8 Minutes, Norwalk Zoning Board of Appeals, April 4, 1940, May 2, 1940.

9 Robert Correia, "City officials urge changes for Norwalk industrial zones." The Norwalk *Hour*, June 23, 1980.

10 Ibid.

11 Minutes, Norwalk Zoning Board of Appeals, April 21, 1955.

12 "Drainage failure protest may get action from the city." The Norwalk *Hour*, December 6, 1955; "Drainage wars occupy the council." The Norwalk *Hour*, December 14, 1955.

13 Transcript, Public Hearing on Up-zoning, Norwalk Planning and Zoning Commission, December 8, 1955.

14 Transcript, Public Hearing on Apartment Regulations, Norwalk Planning and Zoning Commission, April 28, 1955.

15 Transcript, Public Hearing on Up-zoning in West Norwalk, Norwalk Planning and Zoning Commission, February 24, 1955.

16 Transcript, Public Hearing on Up-zoning in Rowayton, Norwalk Planning and Zoning Commission, May 26, 1955.

17 A comparison of the standard deviation of the median family incomes across census tracts for 1960 and 1980 enables us to estimate trends in income inequality across neighborhoods. An increase in the standard deviation (after correction for inflation) from $1428 to $2066 indicates an increase in income inequality during the 1960s and 1970s.

18 Anonymous interviews, Putney Avenue homeowners, Norwalk, August, 1978.

19 In telephone interviews with ten representatives I asked them for an estimate of the number of phone calls concerning the apartment amendment which they received in the week before the July, 1973 meeting. The representatives indicated that almost all of the calls came from their own constituents.

20 Anonymous interview, Westport newspaper reporter, July, 1975.

21 Planning and Zoning Ordinance, 1930; Planning and Zoning Ordinance, Revised edition, 1977, Town of Westport.

22 "You've got trouble, lawyers warn planners." The Westport *News*, November 30, 1977.

23 "Aesthetics win, due to planners' persistence." The Westport *News*, May 11, 1977.

24 Quoted in Andrew O'Connell, "Planners rehash first draft of zoning law." The Westport *News*, May 27, 1977.

25 "Open space subdivision approved by planners." The Westport *News*, April 20, 1977; Andrew O'Connell, "And the builder, pleased, gives his thoughts on planning." The Westport *News*, April 27, 1977.

26 The State of Connecticut requires that towns reassess the value of real estate only once every ten years; in other states where the value of real property must be reassessed each year, local governments are not so dependent on additions to the grand list for annual increments in revenue.

27 Andree Brooks, "Marina conflict troubles Westport." The New York *Times*, August 9, 1978.

28 "Open space subdivision approved by planners." The Westport *News*, April 20, 1977.

29 Jack Bettridge, "Neighbors fume as P & Z decision is delayed." The Westport *News*, September 3, 1980.

30 Jack Bettridge, "Mobile home suit settled out of court." The Westport *News*, December 10, 1980.

31 Source: Minutes of the Westport Planning and Zoning Commission, 1960 and 1970.

32 Jeff Silverstein, "Rezoning moratorium ordered." The Norwalk *Hour*, April 29, 1979.

33 Editorial, "Studies and more studies block progress in Westport." The Westport *News*, December 31, 1976.

34 Source: Minutes, Westport Planning and Zoning Commission, 1979.

35 "Open space study shows little virgin land." The Westport *News*, July 27, 1977.
36 Anonymous interviews, Ryder's Lane homeowners, June, July, 1975.
37 Planners developed estimates of the numbers of in-house apartments in two ways. First, over a period of several years they monitored the local newspapers. Secondly, using building permits and telephone directories, they determined that an in-house apartment had been established at a residence if, shortly after a building permit was issued for the address, another telephone was listed under a separate name for that address.
38 Source: clippings of in-house apartment advertisements, Planning Department, Westport.
39 Andrew O'Connell, "Forum on town's future brings up apartments." The Westport *News*, June 3, 1977.
40 Quoted in Sylvia Porter, "Accessory apartments offer solution to tight housing." The Stamford *Advocate*, June 5, 1982.
41 Jason Isaacon, "Apartment 'crackdown' slows as complaints fall." The Westport *News*, October 13, 1976.
42 Anonymous interview, Ryder's Lane homeowners, May, 1975.
43 As an instance of land-use conversion, the spread of in-house apartments is distinctive in its form. It represents autogenic land-use conversion in that the new type of housing unit appears in neighborhoods only because changes in the households occupying the area cause them to create the new type of housing unit. In this sense the creation of accessory apartments differs from the more commonly cited instances of allogenic land-use conversion in which pressure from an outside group "hastens if it does not start" the change in the pattern of land use. For a discussion of allogenic and autogenic succession see Freudenburg (1985).
44 Anonymous interview, Putney Avenue homeowner, Norwalk, August, 1978.
45 Robert Correia, "Cavenari condo battle nearing agreement." The Norwalk *Hour*, March 4, 1982.
46 "City Hall: the political arena." The Norwalk *Hour*, June 7, 1980.
47 Anonymous interviews, planners, Norwalk, September, 1978.
48 Interview, Ed Leary, Norwalk Planning Director, February, 1986.
49 Anonymous interviews, Putney Avenue homeowners, Norwalk, August, September, 1978.
50 Anonymous interview, Putney Avenue homeowner, Norwalk, August, 1978.
51 Anonymous interviews, Putney Avenue homeowners, Norwalk, August, 1978.
52 Ibid.
53 Anonymous interview, planner, Norwalk, August, 1978.
54 Anonymous interview, planner, Norwalk, June, 1978.
55 Letter, Barry L. Davis to Roy Dickinson, reprinted in the Westport *News*, July 13, 1973.
56 Quoted in Michael Knight, "Westport and its neighbors in a long, simmering feud." The New York *Times*, November 4, 1975.
57 Jeff Silverstein, "Westport bars Norwalk's trash, takes Weston's." The Norwalk *Hour*, March 7, 1979.

58 Quoted in Michael Knight, "Westport and its neighbors."
59 Robert Correia, "Norwalk, Westport battle of SWRPA." The Norwalk *Hour*, June 5, 1979.
60 Joyce Grandinette, "Exclusionary zoning targets of local units." The Norwalk *Hour*, April 8, 1976; Richard L. Madden, "Connecticut woodland aid spurs federal–state debate." The New York *Times*, May 31, 1979.
61 "Silvermine wins its fight.....", op cit.

7 Assessments and applications

1 This argument about the size of jurisdictions can be extended to explain regional differences in both the socio–economic make-up of metropolitan areas and the incidence of conflict between urban communities. Because the larger southern jurisdictions do not produce particularly restrictive controls, the channeling effect, observed in western Connecticut, where wealthy in-migrants move into one community while poor in-migrants move into another community, should not be present to the same degree that it is in the more politically fragmented metropolitan areas of the north. In this manner the size of jurisdications may account for the relative absence of differentiation between communities undergoing suburban development in the south (Logan and Schneider, 1981 : 182). The resulting metropolitan mosaic of land uses, social classes, and races should not be so sharply etched in southern as in northern metropolitan areas. Intense land uses should be more widely scattered instead of clustered in an emerging satellite city. The upper and lower-income tracts should cover wider areas, and the socio-economic differentials between these areas should be less in the south than in the north. Rather than a series of high-income suburbs situated next to lower-middle-income cities, one might find upper-middle and lower-middle-income districts covering larger areas as, for example, in Atlanta with its division into richer northern and poorer southern suburbs or in Houston with its status distinctions between east and west sides (Rice, 1983; Kaplan, 1983:201). By extension one would not expect to find as high an incidence of intercommunity conflict between adjoining communities in the southern and western metropolitan areas as one finds in the northeastern and north central metropolitan areas.
2 Robert E. Tomassen, "Westport approves building of first apartment houses." The New York *Times*, May 18, 1978.
3 Telephone interview, Dave Conine, Local Planning Specialist, State Planning Office, State of Utah, May, 1982.

References

Abbott, Andrew, 1983, "Sequences of social events: concepts and methods for the analysis of order in social processes," *Historical Methods Newsletter* 16(4):129–147

1984, "Event sequence and event duration: colligation and measurement," *Historical Methods Newsletter* 17(4):192–205

Allen, Leslie, Beryl Kuder and Sarah Oakes, 1976, *Promised Lands, I: Subdivisions in Deserts and Mountains*, New York: Inform

1977, *Promised Lands, II: Subdivisions in Florida's Wetlands*. New York: Inform

Alonzo, William, 1965, *Location and Land Use*, Cambridge, Mass.: Harvard University Press

Amir, Shaul, 1972, "Highway location and public opposition," *Environment and Behavior* 4(4):413–436

Austin, James, 1975, "Beverly: subsidized housing and the anti-snob zoning act," in Lawrence Susskind (ed.), *The Land Use Controversy in Massachusetts: Case Studies and Policy Options*, pp. 108–124, Cambridge, Mass.: MIT Press

Axelrod, Robert, 1984, *A Theory of Cooperation*, New York: Basic Books

Babcock, Richard F., 1966, *The Zoning Game*, Madison, Wis.: University of Wisconsin Press

1976, "Regulatory land development: some thoughts on the role of government," in *Land Use: Tough Choices in Today's World*, pp. 32–41, Ankeny, Iowa: Soil Conservation Society of America

Babin, Fred and Barry C. Field, 1977, *Dimensions of Rurality in New England: A Comparative Analysis for the Sixty-seven New England Counties*, Massachusetts Agricultural Experiment Station, #642. Amherst, Mass

Baldassare, Mark and William Protash, 1982, "Growth controls, population growth, and community satisfaction," *American Sociological Review* 47:339–346

Bardach, Eugene and Robert A. Kagan, 1983, *Going by the Book: The Problem of Regulatory Unreasonableness*, Philadelphia: Temple University Press

Barrows, Richard and Carol Olson, 1981, "Soil conservation policy: local actions and federal alternatives," *Journal of Soil and Water Conservation* 36(6):312–316

Beale, Calvin, 1981, "A characterization of types of non-metropolitan areas," in Amos Hawley and Sara Mills Mazie (eds.), *Non-metropolitan America in Transition*, pp. 48–64, Chapel Hill: The University of North Carolina Press

Berger, Jon and J. W. Sinton, 1985, *Water, Earth, and Fire: Land Use and*

Environmental Planning in the New Jersey Pine Barrens, Baltimore: Johns Hopkins University Press

Bernard, L. M. and B. R. Rice (eds.), 1983, *Sunbelt Cities: Politics and Growth since World War II*, Austin, Texas: University of Texas Press

Berry, B. J. L. and John D. Kasarda, 1977, *Contemporary Urban Ecology*, New York: MacMillan

Bingham, Gail, 1985, *Resolving Environmental Disputes: A Decade of Experience*, Washington, DC: Conservation Foundation

Birch, David, 1971, "Towards a stage theory of urban growth," *Journal of the American Institute of Planners* 37(2):78–88

Black, John Donald, 1950, *The Rural Economy of New England*, Cambridge, Mass.: Harvard University Press

Bosselman, Fred, 1979, "The world as a park," in Richard L. Adams (ed.), *Land in America*, Lexington, Mass.: D. C. Heath

Bosselman, Fred, Duayne A. Feurer and Charles H. Sieman, 1976, *The Permit Explosion*, Washington, D.C.: The Urban Institute

Butler, Kent S. and Dowell Myers, 1984, "Boomtime in Austin, Texas," *Journal of the American Planning Association* 50(4):447–458

Caro, Robert, 1974, *The Power Broker: Robert Moses and the Fall of New York*, New York: Random House

Carter, Steve, Murray Frost, Claire Rubin and Lyle Sumak, 1974, *Environmental Management and Local Government*, Washington, D.C.: Environmental Protection Agency

Castells, Manuel, 1977, *The Urban Question*, Cambridge, Mass.: MIT Press
  1983, *The City and the Grassroots*, Berkeley and Los Angeles: University of California Press

Childs, Starling, 1975, *A History of Zoning in Norfolk, Connecticut*, Yale University, unpublished paper

Clavel, Pierre, 1986, *The Progressive City: Planning and Participation, 1969–1986*, New Brunswick, N.J.: Rutgers University Press

Clawson, Marion, 1971, *Suburban Land Conversion in the United States*, Baltimore: Johns Hopkins University Press
  1975, "Environment and land use," *Planning* 41(6):26–28

Coleman, James S., 1966, "Foundations for a theory of collective decisions," *American Journal of Sociology* 71(6):615–623

Conner, Susan, 1981, "Performance zoning: successor to Euclidean zoning." *Land Use Law and Zoning Digest* 33(1):7–10

Corso, Anthony, 1983, "San Diego: the anti-city," in R. M. Bernard and B. R. Rice (eds.), *Sunbelt Cities: Politics and Growth since World War II*, pp. 328–344, Austin, Texas: University of Texas Press

Coughlin, Robert E., Thomas Klein and William Murphy, 1983, *Changes in Patterns of Land Ownership and Use during the Early Stages of Urban Development*, Research Report #1, Department of City and Regional Planning, University of Pennsylvania

Danielson, Michael, 1976, *The Politics of Exclusion*, New York: Columbia University Press

Davidoff, Paul and Mary E. Brooks, 1976, "Zoning out the poor," in P. C. Dolce (ed.), *Suburbia: The American Dream and Dilemma*, pp. 135–166, Garden City, Long Island: Anchor

DeGrove, John M., 1979, "The political dynamics of the land and growth management movement," *Law and Contemporary Problems* 43:111–143

DiMento, Joseph, 1982, "Stressors and the policy sciences," in Gary Evans (ed.), *Stress and the Environment*, Cambridge: Cambridge University Press

Dowall, David, 1984, *The Suburban Squeeze: Land Conversion and Regulation in the San Francisco Bay Area*, Berkeley, Calif.: University of California Press

Downs, Anthony, 1973, *Opening Up the Suburbs*, New Haven: Yale University Press

Eagle, Eva, 1976, *Land Use Planning and Regulation in Arizona's Counties*, Papers in Public Administration, #5, Center for Public Affairs, Arizona State University

Eichler, Ned, 1982, *The Merchant Builders*, Cambridge, Mass.: MIT Press

Elster, Jon, 1982, "Marxism, functionalism, and game theory: the case for methodological individualism," *Theory and Society* 4:453–482

Feagin, Joe R., 1983, *The Urban Real Estate Game*, Englewood Cliffs, N.J.: Prentice-Hall

1985, "The global context of metropolitan growth: Houston and the oil industry," *American Journal of Sociology* 90(6):1204–1230

Firey, Walter, 1947, *Land Use in Central Boston*, Cambridge, Mass.: Harvard University Press

Fischel, William, 1978, "A property rights approach to municipal zoning," *Land Economics* 54(1):64–82

Form, William H., 1954, "The place of social structure in the determination of land use," *Social Forces* 32(4):317–323

Freudenburg, Wm. R., 1985, "Succession and success: a new look at an old concept," *Sociological Spectrum* 5:269–289

Frieden, Bernard J., 1979, *The Environmental Protection Hustle*, Cambridge, Mass.: MIT Press

Garkovich, Lorraine, 1981, "Land use planning as a response to rapid population and community change," *Rural Sociology* 47(1):47–67

Gibbons, Boyd, 1977, *Wye Island: Outsiders and Resistance to Change*, Baltimore: Johns Hopkins University Press

Gibbs, Jack P., 1972, "Social control," A Warner Modular Publication, #1, pp. 1–17, Reading, Mass.: Addison-Wesley

Goetze, Rolf, 1983, *Rescuing the American Dream: Public Policy and the Crisis in Housing*, New York: Holmes and Meier

Goodman, John L., 1978, *Urban Residential Mobility: Places, People, and Policy*, Washington, D.C.: The Urban Institute

Goodman, Robert, 1971, *After the Planners*, New York: Simon and Schuster

Gottdeiner, Mark, 1977, *Planned Sprawl: Public and Private Interests in Suburbia*, Beverly Hills, Calif.: Sage

1985, *The Social Construction of Urban Space*, Austin, Texas: University of Texas Press

Guest, Avery and B. A. Lee, 1983, "The social organization of local areas," *Urban Affairs Quarterly* 19(2):217–240

Guitar, Mary Anne, 1972, *Property Power*, New York: Doubleday

Hamilton, Bruce W., 1978, "Zoning and the exercise of monopoly power," *Journal of Urban Economics* 5(1):116–130

Hardin, Russell, 1982, *Collective Action*, Baltimore: Johns Hopkins University Press

Hartman, Chester, 1974, *Yerba Buena: Land Grab and Community Resistance in San Francisco*, Berkeley, Calif.: National Housing and Economic Development Law Project

1984, *The Transformation of San Francisco*, Totowa, N.J.: Rowman and Allanheld

Harvey, David, 1973, *Social Justice and the City*, Baltimore: Johns Hopkins University Press

1981, "The urban process under capitalism: a framework for analysis," in M. Dear and A. Scott (eds.), *Urbanization and Urban Planning in Capitalist Society*, New York: Methuen

Hawkins, Keith, 1984, *Environment and Enforcement: Regulation and the Social Definition of Pollution*, Oxford: Clarendon Press

Hawkins, Robert B., 1975, "Local land use planning and its critics," in *No Man Is an Island*, San Francisco: Institute for Contemporary Studies

Hawley, Amos, 1950, *Human Ecology: A Theory of Community Structure*, New York: Ronald Press

Healy, Robert G. and John S. Rosenberg, 1979, *Land Use and the States*, Second edition, Baltimore: Johns Hopkins University Press

Hirschman, Albert O., 1973, "The changing tolerance for income inequality during the course of economic development," *Quarterly Journal of Economics* 87:544–566

Holcomb, H. Briavel and R. A. Beaureguard, 1981, *Revitalizing Cities*, Washington, D.C.: Association of American Geographers

Iowa, Office of Planning and Programming, 1977, *Local Land Use Controls in Iowa: a Survey and Analysis*

Kaplan, B. J., 1983, "Houston: the golden buckle of the sunbelt," in R. M. Bernard and B. R. Rice (eds.), pp. 196–212, *Sunbelt Cities*, Austin, Texas: University of Texas Press

Kaplan, Samuel, 1976, *The Dream Deferred: People, Politics, and Planning in Suburbia*, New York: Seabury

Kasarda, J. D. and M. Janowitz, 1974, "Community attachment in mass society," *American Sociological Review* 39(6):328–3

Kenney, Kenneth B., 1972, "The residential land developer and his land purchase decision," Environmental Policies and Urban Development Thesis Series #16, Chapel Hill, North Carolina: Center for Urban and Regional Studies

Krannich, R. S. and C. R. Humphrey, 1983, "Local mobilization and community growth: toward an assessment of the 'growth machine' hypothesis," *Rural Sociology* 48(1):60–81

Lassey, William R., 1977, *Planning in Rural Environments*, New York: McGraw-Hill

Lasswell, Harold, 1936, *Politics: Who Gets What, When, and How?* New York: McGraw-Hill

Law Enforcement Assistance Administration, 1979, *Corruption in Land Use and Building Regulation, Vol. 1: An Integrated Report of Conclusions*, Washington, D.C.: Government Printing Office

Lemire, Robert A., 1979, *Creative Land Development: Bridge to the Future*, Boston: Houghton–Mifflin

Liebrand, W. B., 1983, "A classification of social dilemma games," *Simulation and Games* 14(2):123–138

Logan, John R., 1976a, "Industrialization and the stratification of cities in suburban regions," *American Journal of Sociology* 82:333–348

  1976b, "Notes on the growth machine: toward a political economy of place," *American Journal of Sociology* 82:349–352

Logan, John R. and Mark Schneider, 1981, "The stratification of metropolitan suburbs, 1960–1970," *American Sociological Review* 46(2):175–186

Long, John F., 1981, *Population Deconcentration in the United States*, Special Demographic Analysis, CDS-81-5, Washington, D.C.: Government Printing Office

Long, Norton, 1958, "The local community as an ecology of games," *American Journal of Sociology* 61(2):251–261

Lorimer, James, 1972, *A Citizen's Guide to City Politics*, Toronto: James Lewis and Samuel

  1979, *The Developers*, Toronto: James Lorimer and Co

Lynch, Kevin, 1981, *The Theory of Good City Form*, Cambridge, Mass.: MIT Press

Lyon, Larry, L. G. Felice, M. R. Perryman and E. S. Parker, 1981, "Community power and population increase: an empirical test of the growth machine model," *American Journal of Sociology* 86(6):1387–1400

McBride, G. A. and Marion Clawson, 1970, "Negotiation and land conversion," *Journal of the American Institute of Planners* 36(1):22–29

McGranahan, David A., 1984, "Local growth and the outside contacts of influentials: an alternative test of the growth machine hypothesis," *Rural Sociology* 49(4):530–540

MacNeil, I. R., 1974, "The many futures of contracts," *University of Southern California Law Review* 67:691–816

  1978, "Contracts: adjustment of longterm economic relations under classical, neoclassical, and relational contract law," *Northwestern University Law Review* 72:854–902

Mansbridge, Jane, 1980, *Beyond Adversary Democracy*, New York: Free Press

Maurer, R. C. and James Christenson, 1982, "Growth and nongrowth orientations of urban, suburban, and rural mayors: reflections on the city as a growth machine," *Social Science Quarterly* 63:350–358

Maynard Smith, John, 1982, *Evolution and the Theory of Games*, Cambridge: Cambridge University Press

Minnesota, State Planning Agency, 1981, *A Study of Local Efforts to Manage Land Use in Minnesota*

Molotch, Harvey, 1976, "The city as a growth machine: toward a political economy of place," *American Journal of Sociology* 82:309–332

1979, "Capital and neighborhood in the United States: some conceptual links," *Urban Affairs Quarterly* 14(3):289–313

Molotch, Harvey and John Logan, 1984, "Tensions in the growth machine," *Social Problems* 31(5):483–499

Morath, Inge and Arthur Miller, 1977, *In the Country*, New York: Viking

Morganstern, Oskar, 1968, "Game theory: theoretical aspects," in D. Sills (ed.), *International Encyclopedia of the Social Sciences, Vol. 6*, pp. 61–68, New York: MacMillan

Nader Study Group on Land Use in California, 1973, *Politics of Land*, New York: Grossman

Nelkin, Dorothy, 1974, *Jetport: the Boston Airport Controversy*, New Brunswick, N.J.: Transaction Books

Nellis, Lee, 1980, "Planning with rural values," *Journal of Soil and Water Conservation* 35:67–71

Nelson, Robert H., 1978, *Zoning and Property Rights*, Cambridge, Mass.: MIT Press

de Neufville, Judith Innes, 1982, "Land use: a tool for social policies," in Judith Innes de Neufville (ed.), *The Land Use Policy Debate in the United States*, pp. 31–47, New York: Plenum

New Hampshire Fish and Game Department, 1971, *Land Posting in New Hampshire*, Concord, N.H.

Olson, Mancur, 1965, *The Logic of Collective Action*, Cambridge, Mass.: Harvard University Press

1982, *The Rise and Decline of Nations: Economic Growth, Stagflation, and Social Rigidities*, New Haven and London: Yale University Press

Orbell, John and L. A. Wilson, 1978, "Institutional solutions to the n-person prisoner's dilemma," *American Political Science Review* 72:411–421

Ostrom, Elinor, 1983, "The social stratification – government inequality thesis explored," *Urban Affairs Quarterly* 19(1):91–112

Park, R., E. Burgess, and R. MacKenzie, 1925, *The City*, Chicago: University of Chicago Press

Parker, R. A., T. Airola, B. Chavooshian and G. Nieswand, 1984, *Commercial Restructuring at the Rural–Urban Fringe*, New Jersey Agricultural Experiment Station, Report #17412

Peiser, Richard P., 1981, "Land development regulation: a case study of Dallas and Houston, Texas," *Journal of the American Real Estate and Urban Economics Association* 9:397–417

Popper, Frank J., 1981, *The Politics of Land Use Reform*, Madison, Wis.: University of Wisconsin Press

Rabinowitz, Francine, 1969, *City Planning and Politics*, New York: Atherton

Reilly, William (ed.), 1973, *The Use of Land*, New York: Crowell

Reps, John W., 1972, "Pomeroy Memorial Lecture: requiem for zoning," in Richard Andrews (ed.), *Urban Land Use Policy*, pp. 10–18, New York: Free Press

Rice, B. R., 1983, "If Dixie were Atlanta." Pp. 31–57 in B. R. Rice and R. M. Bernard (eds.), *Sunbelt Cities*, Austin, Texas: University of Texas Press

Rosenbaum, Nelson, 1976, *Land Use and the Legislatures: the Politics of State Innovation*, Washington, D.C.: The Urban Institute

Rudel, Thomas K., 1980, "The quiet revolution in municipal land use control," *Journal of Environmental Management* 10(1):125–137

    1984a, "The human ecology of rural land use planning," *Rural Sociology* 49(4):491–504

    1984b, "Household change, accessory apartments, and low income housing in suburbs," *Professional Geographer* 36(2):174–181

Salter, J. F., 1981, *Shadow Forks: A Small Community's Relation to Ecology and Regulation*, PhD Dissertation, University of California–Santa Cruz

Schlay, Ann and Peter Rossi, 1981, "Keeping up the neighborhood: estimating the net effects of zoning," *American Sociological Review* 46(6):703–719

Schmid, A. A., 1970, "Suburban land appreciation and public policy," *Journal of the American Institute of Planners* 36(1):38–43

Schnaiberg, Allan, 1984, "Movements in the Sands," *Contemporary Sociology* 13(4):415–417

Schneider, Mark and John R. Logan, 1982, "Fiscal implications of class segregation: inequalities in the distribution of public goods and services in suburban municipalities," *Urban Affairs Quarterly* 17(3):23–37

Scholz, John T., 1984, "Cooperation, deterrence, and the ecology of regulatory enforcement," *Law and Society Review* 18(2):179–224

Scott, Allen, 1980, *The Urban Land Nexus and the State*, London: Pion

Socolow, Alvin D., 1968, *Government Response to Urbanization: Three Townships on the Rural–urban Fringe*, Report #132, Economics Research Service, USDA, Washington, D.C.

Spectorsky, A. C., 1955, *The Exurbanites*, Philadelphia: Lippincott

Strong, Ann, 1975, *Private Property and the Public Interest*, Baltimore: Johns Hopkins University Press

Susskind, Lawrence, 1982, "Citizen participation and consensus building in land use planning: a case study," in Judith Innes de Neufville, *The Land Use Policy Debate in the United States*, pp. 183–204, New York: Plenum

Talbot, Allan R., 1983, *Settling Things: Six Case Studies in Environmental Mediation*, Washington, D.C.: The Conservation Foundation

Tarrant, John J., 1976, *The End of Exurbia*, New York: Day & Co

Thompson, Edward, 1980, *Farming in the Shadow of Suburbia: Case Studies in Agricultural Land Use Conflict*, Washington, D.C.: National Association of Counties Research Foundation

Warwick, Donald P. and Charles A. Lininger, 1975, *The Sample Survey: Theory and Practice*, New York: McGraw-Hill

Weaver, Clifford L. and Richard F. Babcock, 1980, *City Zoning: The Once and Future Frontier*, Chicago, Ill.: American Planning Association

Whetten, Norman, 1942, *Studies of Suburbanization in Connecticut*, Storrs, Conn.: Agricultural Experiment Station

Whetten, N. and R. Rapaport, 1936, *The Recreational Use of Land in Connecticut*, Storrs, Conn.: Agricultural Experiment Station, Bulletin 194

Willhelm, Sidney, 1962, *Urban Zoning and Land Use Theory*, Glencoe, Ill.: Free Press

Williams, Norman Jr. and Thomas Norman, 1974, "Evolutionary land use controls: the case of northeastern New Jersey," in *Land Use Controls: Present Problems and Future Reform*, New Brunswick, N.J.: Center for Urban Policy Research

Williamson, O. E. 1975, *Markets and Hierarchies*, New York: Free Press

1979, "Transaction cost economics: the governance of contractual relations," Journal of Law and Economics 22:233–261

1981, "The economics of organization: the transaction cost approach," *American Journal of Sociology* 87(3):548–577

Wood, Robert C., 1961, *1400 Governments*, Cambridge, Mass.: Harvard University Press

Yates, Douglas, 1977, *The Ungovernable City: The Politics of Urban Problems and Policy Making*, Cambridge, Mass.: MIT Press

Zagare, Frank C., 1984, *Game Theory: Concepts and Applications*, Beverly Hills and London: Sage

Zeigler, Donald J. and Stanley D. Brunn, 1980, "Geopolitical fragmentation and the pattern of growth and need: defining the cleavage between sunbelt and frostbelt metropolises," in Stanley D. Brunn and James O. Wheeler (eds.), The *American Metropolitan System: Present and Future*, pp. 77–92, New York: John Wiley

Index

Other books in the series

J. Milton Yinger, Kiyoshi Ikeda, Frank Laycock, and Stephen J. Cutler: *Middle Start: An Experiment in the Educational Enrichment of Young Adolescents*

James A. Geschwender: *Class, Race, and Worker Insurgency: The League of Revolutionary Black Workers*

Paul Ritterband: *Education, Employment, and Migration: Israel in Comparative Perspective*

John Low-Beer: *Protest and Participation: The New Working Class in Italy*

Orrin E. Klapp: *Opening and Closing: Strategies of Information Adaptation in Society*

Rita James Simon: *Continuity and Change: A Study of Two Ethnic Communities in Israel*

Marshall B. Clinard: *Cities with Little Crime: The Case of Switzerland**

Steven T. Bossert: *Tasks and Social Relationships in Classrooms: A Study of Instructional Organization and Its Consequences*

Richard E. Johnson: *Juvenile Delinquency and Its Origins: An Integrated Theoretical Approach**

David R. Heise: *Understanding Events: Affect and the Construction of Social Action*

Ida Harper Simpson: *From Student to Nurse: A Longitudinal Study of Socialization*

Stephen P. Turner: *Sociological Explanation as Translation*

Janet W. Salaff: *Working Daughters of Hong Kong: Filial Piety or Power in the Family?*

Joseph Chamie: *Religion and Fertility: Arab Christian-Muslim Differentials*

William Friedland, Amy Barton, Robert Thomas: *Manufacturing Green Gold: Capital, Labor, and Technology in the Lettuce Industry*

Richard N. Adams: *Paradoxical Harvest: Energy and Explanation in British History, 1870–1914*

Mary F. Rogers: *Sociology, Ethnomethodology, and Experience: A Phenomenological Critique*

James R. Beniger: *Trafficking in Drug Users: Professional Exchange Networks in the Control of Deviance*

* *Available from American Sociological Association, 1722 N Street, N.W., Washington, DC 20036.*

165

Andrew J. Weigert, J. Smith Teitge, and Denis W. Teitge: *Society and Identity: Toward a Sociological Psychology*

Jon Miller: *Pathways in the Workplace: The Effects of Race and Gender on Access to Organizational Resources*

Michael A. Faia: *Dynamic Functionalism: Strategy and Tactics*

Joyce Rothschild and J. Allen Whitt: *The Co-operative Workplace: Potentials and Dilemmas of Organizational Democracy*

Russell Thornton: *We Shall Live Again: The 1870 and 1890 Ghost Dance Movements as Demographic Revitalization*

Severyn T. Bruyn: *The Field of Social Investment*

Guy E. Swanson: *Ego Defenses and the Legitimation of Behavior*

Liah Greenfeld: *Different worlds: a Sociological Study of Taste, Choice and Success in Art*